W9-AYG-325

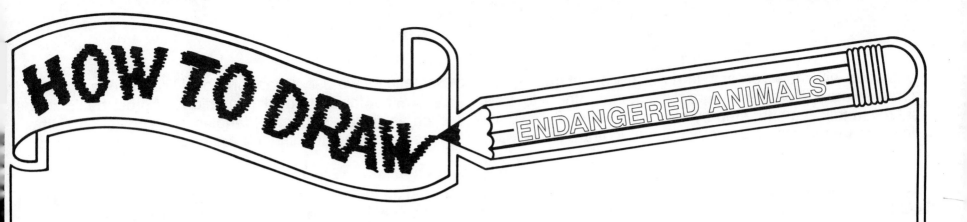

Illustrated by Georgene Griffin

Copyright © 1996 Kidsbooks Inc.
3535 West Peterson Avenue
Chicago, IL 60659

All rights reserved including the right
of reproduction in whole or in part in any form.

Manufactured in the United States of America

Visit us at www.kidsbooks.com
Volume discounts available for group purchases.

INTRODUCTION

This book will show you how to draw lots of different endangered animals. Some are more difficult than others to draw, but if you follow along, step-by-step, you'll soon be able to draw these and others as you continue to learn about wildlife in danger.

The most basic shape used to draw these animals is the common oval. There are many variations of the oval—some are small and round, others are long and flat, and many are in-between. Each figure in this book begins with a type of oval. Then, other ovals, shapes, and lines are added to round out the basic sections of the body.

Sometimes we use a free-form oval like the ones pictured below. In addition to ovals, variations of other basic shapes, such as circles, squares, triangles, rectangles, and simple lines to connect the shapes are used.

Using these basic shapes will help you start your drawing. These shapes, in different sizes and combinations, will change from animal to animal. Remember, many variations of these basic shapes will also be used throughout the book.

Some basic oval shapes:

Free form

Free form

SUPPLIES

NUMBER 2 PENCILS
SOFT ERASER
DRAWING PAD
COLORED PENCILS, MARKERS,
OR CRAYONS

HELPFUL HINTS

Following the first two steps carefully will make the final eps easier.

Always keep your pencil lines light and soft. These guidelines" will be easier to erase when you no longer need em.

Don't be afraid to erase. It usually takes lots of drawing and rasing before you will be satisfied with the way your endanered animal looks.

4. Add details and all the finishing touches **after** you have blended and refined all the shapes and your figure is complete.

5. Remember: **Practice Makes Perfect.** Don't be discouraged if you can't get the "hang of it" right away. Just keep drawing and erasing until you do.

The first two steps create a **solid foundation** of the figure—much like a builder who must first construct a foundation before building the rest of the house. Next comes the fun part—creating the smooth outline drawing of the animal, and adding all the details, finishing touches, and shading.

3

HOW TO START

Practice drawing the *black-footed ferret* below before going ahead.

1. Begin by drawing the oval shapes like the ones in step 1. Note how the ovals overlap.

2. Beginning with the overlapping oval that forms the neck and head, add the other shapes to the first ones. Note that many of these ovals and shapes are not "perfect." These are the basic guidelines that form the body and create the foundation.

REMEMBER TO KEEP YOUR LINES LIGHTLY DRAWN

3. Carefully blend and combine all the shapes and lines into a smooth outline drawing of the ferret. The dotted lines show what can be erased as you go along. When you are satisfied with your drawing, and all the guidelines you no longer need have been erased, you're ready for the finishing touches.

4. Add the facial features, other details and texture, fur and ha and shading to complete your endangered animal drawing. Color your finished endangered animal or, for a more dramati effect, use less shading and outline your drawing with a thick, black marker.

Use your **imagination** and draw different backgrounds to enhance your drawings.
Create a complete scene by adding other animals that live in the same habitat.

When you have drawn some or all of the animals in this book and are comfortable with the drawing technique, you should able to draw any animal you wish, not only the endangered ones.

Most of all, **HAVE FUN!**

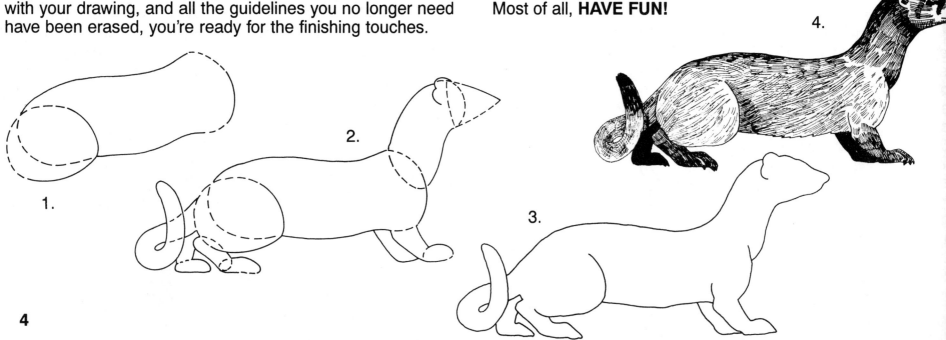

1.

2.

3.

4.

ABOUT ENDANGERED ANIMALS

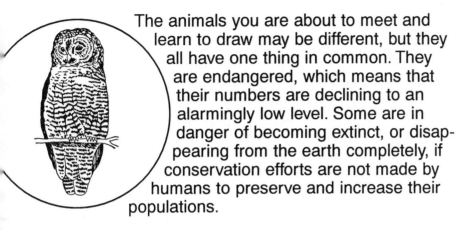

The animals you are about to meet and learn to draw may be different, but they all have one thing in common. They are endangered, which means that their numbers are declining to an alarmingly low level. Some are in danger of becoming extinct, or disappearing from the earth completely, if conservation efforts are not made by humans to preserve and increase their populations.

Why are they endangered?

There are many different reasons why a group of animals becomes endangered or threatened. Usually, it happens from natural changes in the earth over time or from the effect people have on nature. Sometimes animals become endangered if a sudden disease strikes and spreads.

Over thousands or millions of years many animals become extinct. Sixty-five million years ago dinosaurs disappeared from the earth. But scientists estimate that dinosaur species died off at the rate of only one species per 1,000 years. Today, it is estimated that nearly 1,000 plant and animal species become extinct each year! In the last 300 years, over 300 vertebrates (animals with backbones) have become extinct.

Humans have changed the world at a rapid pace. As the human population grows, people need more and more land for

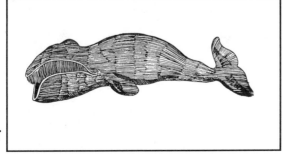

farms, homes, roads, and cities. Trees, and sometimes whole forests, are cut down, causing animals to lose their habitats and source of food. Air and water pollution also takes its toll. Hunters and trappers seek out certain animals for food, skins and furs, and valuable trophies. This has caused many species to face extinction much sooner than they might on nature's own time.

What's being done?

Now, more than ever, people are becoming aware of the plight of endangered animals, and a greater effort is being made worldwide to preserve the earth's wild resources.

• Conservationists are increasing endangered species populations by breeding and raising them in captivity.

The American alligator, bison, and bald eagle are species that have returned from the brink of extinction to the point where they are no longer considered endangered. The alligator was trapped for its valuable skin. The bison was hunted for food and sport, while the bald eagle became rare because the fish they fed on contained the pesticide DDT. This chemical made the eagle's eggshells so thin that fewer and fewer eaglets were being born.

Today, thanks to the efforts of concerned people, DDT is banned and the bald eagles are back. Herds of bison once again roam areas of the American West and the alligator population has almost completely recovered.

One thing *you* can do to help endangered animals is to learn about them—and you can begin right here as you also learn how to draw them.

• When possible, endangered animals are being reintroduced to their natural habitat.

• Protected lands—national parks and animal preserves—have been set aside for animals to live without the threat of being hunted.

• Hunting is now regulated in most areas.

• People are being educated about the vital role all living things play on our delicately balanced planet.

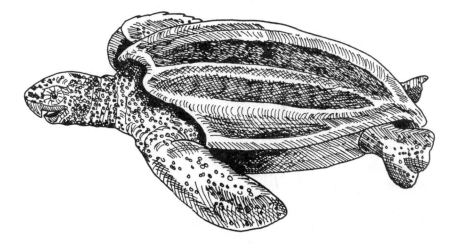

West Indian Manatee

This shy, gentle water mammal is also known as the Sea Cow. Spending its entire life in warm, sheltered waters, a 12-foot manatee can eat up to 100 pounds of vegetation daily. Manatees can weigh up to 3,000 pounds but have a 1-pound brain!

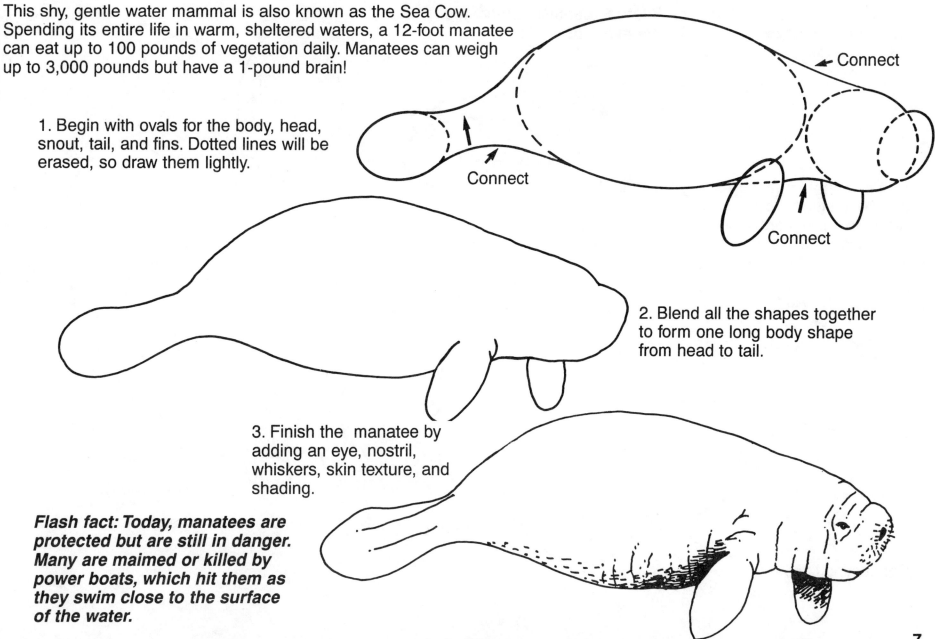

1. Begin with ovals for the body, head, snout, tail, and fins. Dotted lines will be erased, so draw them lightly.

Connect

Connect

Connect

2. Blend all the shapes together to form one long body shape from head to tail.

3. Finish the manatee by adding an eye, nostril, whiskers, skin texture, and shading.

Flash fact: Today, manatees are protected but are still in danger. Many are maimed or killed by power boats, which hit them as they swim close to the surface of the water.

Bactrian Camel

*Flash fact: Only a few hundred Bactrian camels survive today.
One calf is born to an adult female every other year.*

1. Start with a large, egg-shaped oval for the body. Add smaller ovals for the humps and head. Be sure to draw the basic shapes and connecting lines lightly. These guidelines will be erased later.

Add

Add

Connecting lines

Connecting lines

2. Next, add more oval shapes for the legs and feet. Draw the tail as shown.

3. Blend all the roughed-out shapes into one body frame. Remember to erase any lines you no longer need.

4. Add important details such as the eye, ear, nose, and mouth. Complete your camel by giving its coat a shaggy look.

Keep erasing and drawing until you are satisfied.

Tiger

The biggest of all cats, tigers live only in Asia. Although overhunted for its beautiful coat, the tiger's greatest threat is loss of habitat. There are five times as many people living in the areas roamed by tigers than there were in 1900.

2. Add ovals for the paws and connect them to the body, forming the legs. Add long, graceful lines for the tail.

Taper and curve tail

1. Draw a circle for the shoulder area and two ovals for the hindquarter and head. Connect the three shapes. Add the ears and lower part of the face as shown.

3. Next, blend and shape all the lines into a sleek tiger's body. Erase any guidelines you no longer need.

Add lines for toes

4. To complete your drawing, add the tiger's facial features, famous stripes, and other details.

Flash fact: Between 1900 and 1970 about 95,000 tigers were killed. Project Tiger was started by the World Wildlife Fund in 1973 when there were only 5,000 tigers left. Today, the number of tigers continues to decline as they are hunted for use in medical science.

Giant Anteater

More and more South American grasslands are being grazed by cattle. This means fewer and fewer termite mounds, home to the giant anteater's favorite food.

Note: It's usually easier to begin each drawing by sketching the largest shape first.

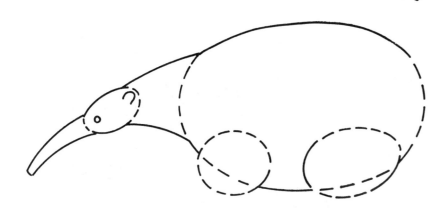

1. Lightly sketch an oval shape for the body and two overlapping ovals for the shoulder and thigh. Draw a small oval for the head and connect it to the body. Add the eye and ear and a long, slender snout to the head.

2. Add more guidelines for the legs and paws, and a large free-form oval for the huge, bushy tail. Now that the basic shapes have been completed, you can begin to refine your drawing.

Flash fact: The giant anteater's sticky, 24-inch-long tongue is perfect for picking up ants and termites. It can eat up to 30,000 of these insects in one day!

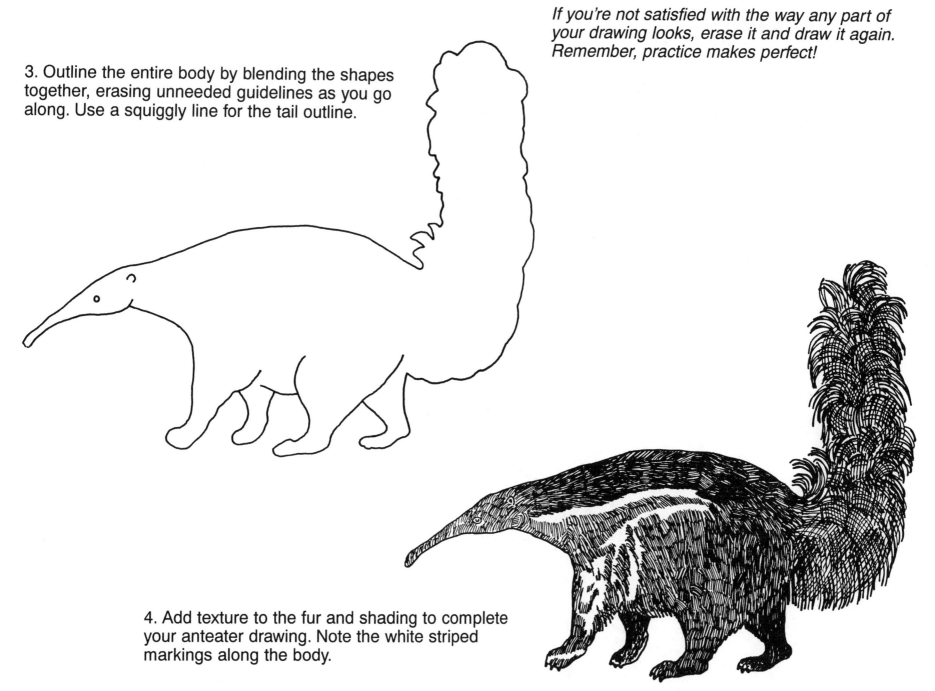

3. Outline the entire body by blending the shapes together, erasing unneeded guidelines as you go along. Use a squiggly line for the tail outline.

If you're not satisfied with the way any part of your drawing looks, erase it and draw it again. Remember, practice makes perfect!

4. Add texture to the fur and shading to complete your anteater drawing. Note the white striped markings along the body.

13

Giant Panda

Giant pandas are very rare animals that live only in the forests of central China. They grow to 6 feet and can weigh 300 pounds. These gentle animals are vegetarians and consume 25 pounds of bamboo shoots and stems daily.

Connect

Connect

1. Draw a large oval for the panda's body, and smaller ones for the head, snout, nose, and ears.

2. Add oval guidelines for the legs and paws.

Note: Always draw guidelines lightly. If you don't like the way something looks, erase and try again.

3. Add the mouth, eye patches, and shape the nose. Blend and curve all lines into a complete body shape. Erase any guidelines you no longer need.

Add eye patches

Flash fact: Fewer than 1,000 pandas remain in China's mountain bamboo forests. The giant panda is the emblem of the World Wildlife Fund, an organization that protects rare animals and plants.

4. Draw the eyes and nose details. Then, add the finishing touch by shading the panda's fur. Draw the giant panda munching on its favorite food—bamboo.

Eskimo Curlew

These birds migrate all the way from Alaska
to Chile and back again each year.
So many have been killed by hunters
that for awhile curlews were thought to be extinct.

*Note: Always draw your guidelines lightly
in steps 1 and 2. It will be easier to change
or erase them later.*

2. Add a long, curved beak to the head,
and the other guideline shapes for the legs
and feet, as shown. Erase any guidelines
you no longer need as you go along.

1. Begin by lightly sketching a large
oval guideline shape, creating the
body. Then, draw a small circle for
the head and a tiny circle for the
eye. Connect the shapes and add
the triangular shapes for the tail
feathers.

Flash fact: Although hunting has now been banned, it may be too late to save the curlews.

4. Complete the eye and add shading to the beak and legs. Define the short body feathers before shading them in.

3. Start blending the shapes into a smooth outline of the curlew. Pay special attention to the legs and feet. When you're satisfied with the way your drawing looks, you're ready for the final details.

17

Asian Elephant

Smaller than its African cousin—with smaller tusks and ears—this highly intelligent animal is still used as a work animal in Southeast Asia. Its numbers have been rapidly diminishing due to overhunting and loss of habitat.

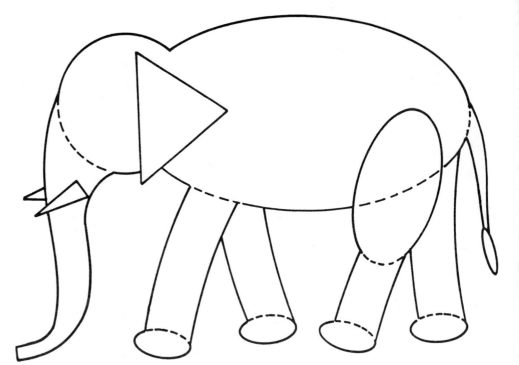

2. Next, add long, curved lines for the trunk and tail, and triangles for the tusks and ear.

Connect →

1. Start with a large oval guideline for the elephant's body. Add a circle for the head and an oval for the hindquarter. Add ovals for the feet and connect them to the body.

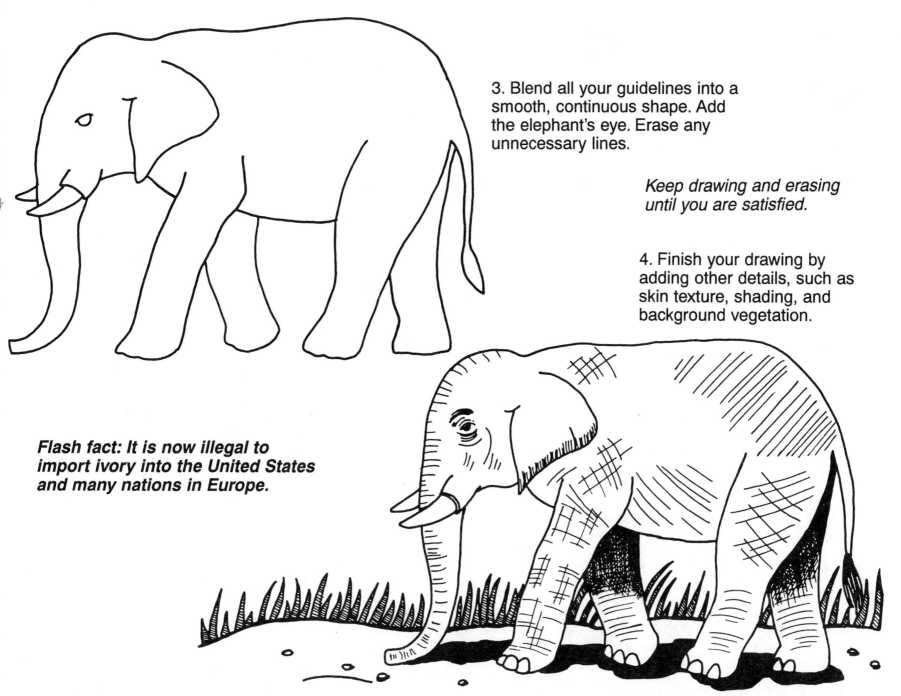

3. Blend all your guidelines into a smooth, continuous shape. Add the elephant's eye. Erase any unnecessary lines.

Keep drawing and erasing until you are satisfied.

4. Finish your drawing by adding other details, such as skin texture, shading, and background vegetation.

Flash fact: It is now illegal to import ivory into the United States and many nations in Europe.

Komodo Dragon

The largest of the monitor lizards living today, the Komodo dragon is a 10-foot long, 300-pound reptile that lives on the island of Komodo and on a few other small Indonesian islands.

Draw all the lines lightly in steps one and two. They are only guidelines and will be erased.

2. Add oval and rectangle guidelines for one foreleg (the other is hidden from view). Add two long, curved lines for the tail—as long as the head and body combined.

1. Begin by drawing a large oval for the body and a smaller oval for the head. Next, draw ovals and rectangles for the hind legs.

3. Add the toes, and round and blend all guidelines into one body form until you're satisfied with your drawing.

← Taper

4. Add the mouth, eye, nostrils, claws, and a long, forked tongue. Light, criss-crossed lines give the skin a wrinkly texture. Add some shading for the finishing touch.

Flash fact: Komodo dragons have no known enemies on their native islands—man has been the only threat to their existence.

Brown Hyena

This scavenger is found in the south of Africa. The brown hyena competes for food, mostly unsuccessfully, with its bigger cousin, the spotted hyena.

Note: Steps 1 and 2 are very important. They establish the basic overall structure and look of your drawing. In steps 3 and 4 you are simply refining and adding details to the figure you have created in steps 1 and 2.

2. Add the guideline shapes for the legs, paws, and big bushy tail.

1. Begin by lightly drawing the large free-form oval for the body. Then add the simple shapes for the head, face, and ears.

Flash fact: Many hyenas are killed by farmers who consider them a threat to their farm animals.

3. Blend the shapes together and keep erasing your guidelines as you continue to refine the figure.

4. Add all the final details and shading to the hyena's face and body. Note the dark rings of shading on the legs. Don't forget the whiskers.

Malayan Tapir

Tapirs are a kind of cross betweena horse and a rhinoceros. A baby Malayan tapir has a black-and-white spotted coat. As it grows older, it becomes half black (front end) and half white (back end).

Remember: It's easy to draw almost anything if you first build a good foundation.

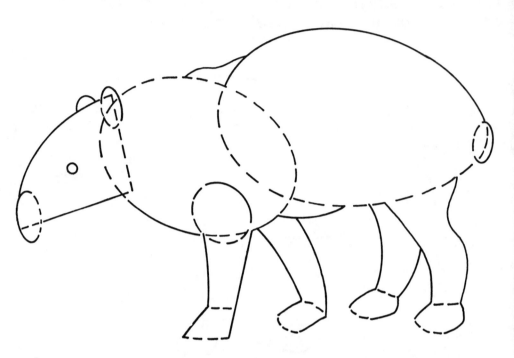

2. Add the basic guideline shapes for the head, along with the shapes for the ears, eye, and nose. Then sketch in the shapes for the legs and feet.

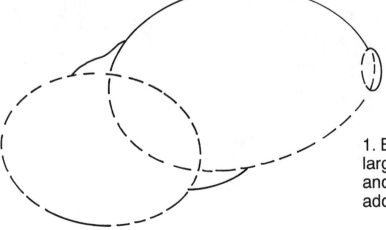

1. Begin by lightly sketching two large, overlapping ovals for the body, and connecting them as shown. Then add a small oval for the tail.

24

Flash fact: The leaf-eating tapir is endangered due to destruction of its forest habitat in Borneo and Malaya.

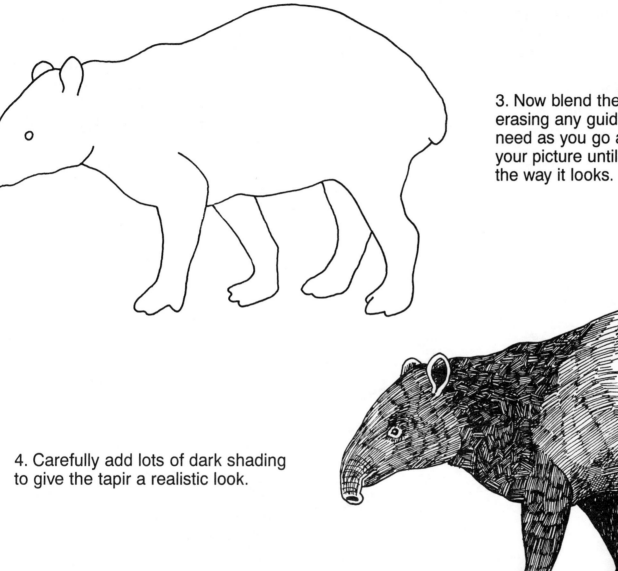

3. Now blend the shapes together, erasing any guidelines you no longer need as you go along. Keep refining your picture until you're satisfied with the way it looks.

4. Carefully add lots of dark shading to give the tapir a realistic look.

Numbat

Found in the southwest corner of Australia, the numbat dines only on termites. Loss of habitat to farming, and being preyed upon by foxes and dogs, has seriously reduced the number of numbats.

Remember to draw these guidelines lightly.
They will be easier to erase as you refine and complete your picture.

1. Begin by drawing a large, irregular oval shape for the body. Add a pear shape for the head and the other basic shapes for the eye, ears, nose, and mouth.

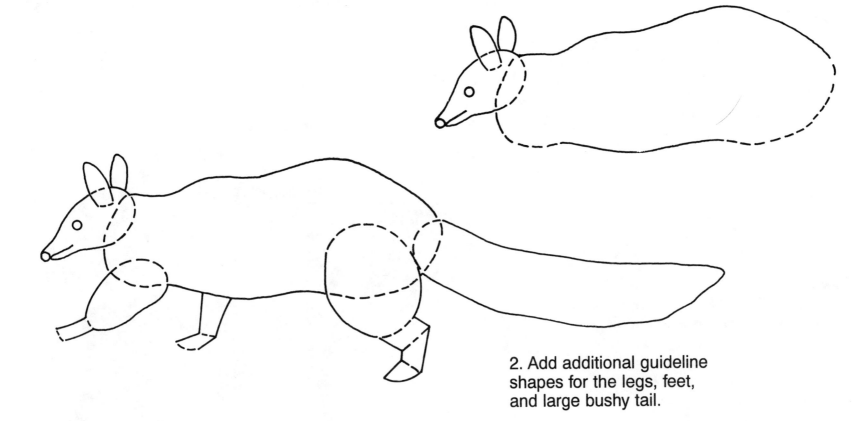

2. Add additional guideline shapes for the legs, feet, and large bushy tail.

Flash fact: Like kangaroos and koalas, the numbat is a marsupial. The babies are raised in their mother's pouch.

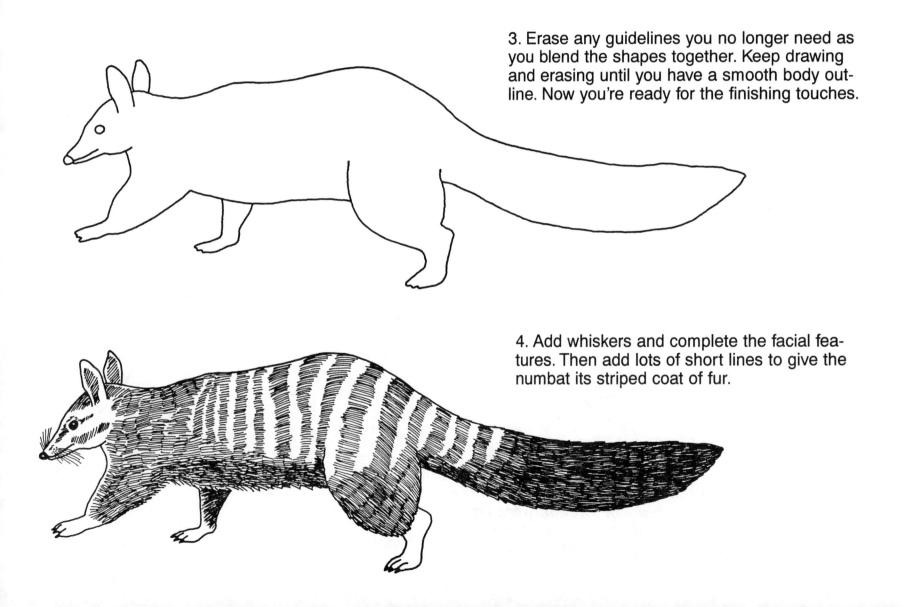

3. Erase any guidelines you no longer need as you blend the shapes together. Keep drawing and erasing until you have a smooth body outline. Now you're ready for the finishing touches.

4. Add whiskers and complete the facial features. Then add lots of short lines to give the numbat its striped coat of fur.

Red Wolf

Because wolves were greatly feared by farmers and ranchers, many of these striking animals were shot, trapped, and poisoned. The natural habitats of red wolves—areas with heavy vegetative cover—are shrinking dramatically.

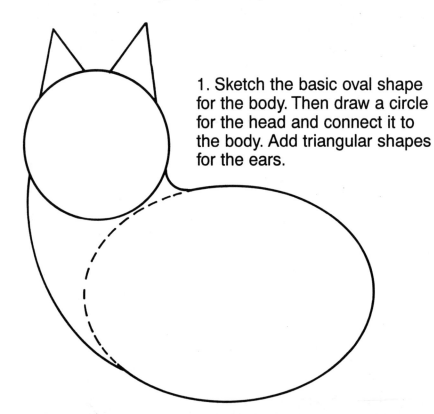

1. Sketch the basic oval shape for the body. Then draw a circle for the head and connect it to the body. Add triangular shapes for the ears.

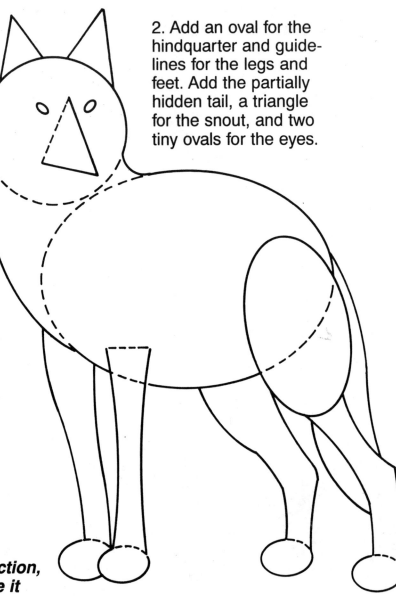

2. Add an oval for the hindquarter and guidelines for the legs and feet. Add the partially hidden tail, a triangle for the snout, and two tiny ovals for the eyes.

Flash fact: As hunters almost drove them toward extinction, the remaining red wolves bred with coyotes. For awhile it was suspected that no pure red wolf breeds were left. However, some of those that still exist are raised in zoos, while others have been released in protected preserves.

3. Combine the basic shapes into a complete body outline. Erase any guidelines you no longer need.

4. Finish the eyes, nose, and other facial details. Use short, irregular lines and shading to give your wolf a "furry" look.

Mountain Gorilla

A small area in Africa is the last home of these shy and gentle primates. The rapid destruction of the forests in which they live forces the gorillas to move farther and farther into remote areas.

1. Start by drawing three ovals as guides for the head, shoulder area, and hindquarters. Connect them to each other. Then add the arms and hands.

2. Add ovals for the legs and feet.

Work on each section of the gorilla separately. If you're not satisfied with the way any part looks, erase it and start over again.

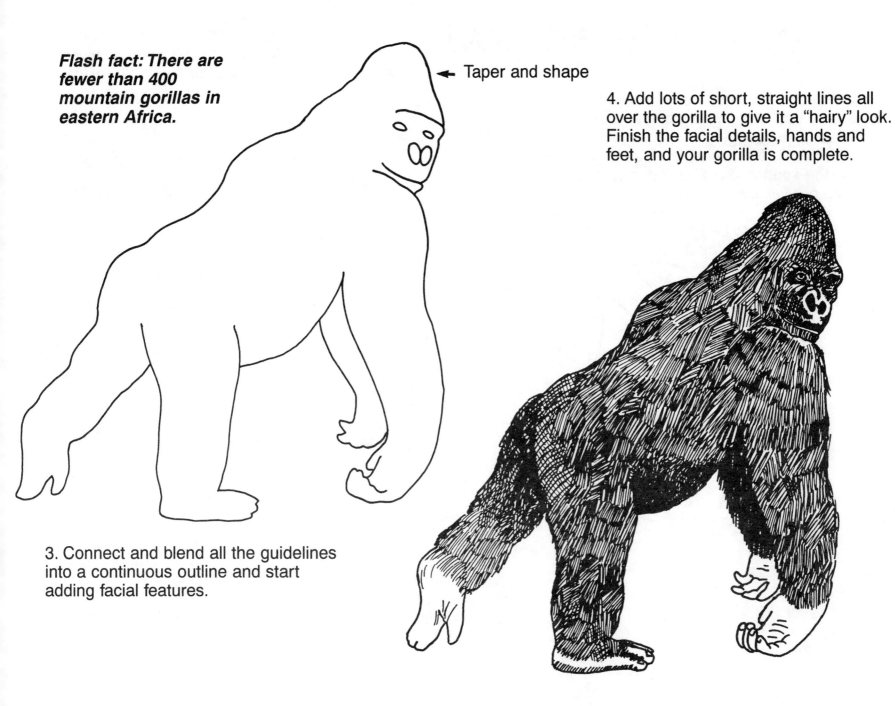

Flash fact: There are fewer than 400 mountain gorillas in eastern Africa.

← Taper and shape

4. Add lots of short, straight lines all over the gorilla to give it a "hairy" look. Finish the facial details, hands and feet, and your gorilla is complete.

3. Connect and blend all the guidelines into a continuous outline and start adding facial features.

Northern Spotted Owl

The northern spotted owl has been involved in a controversy between timber companies and conservationists. Logging produces jobs and money for the Pacific Northwest. That same logging is destroying the spotted owl's habitat, and if it continues, the owl will become extinct.

Note: It's usually easier to begin each drawing by sketching the largest shape first.

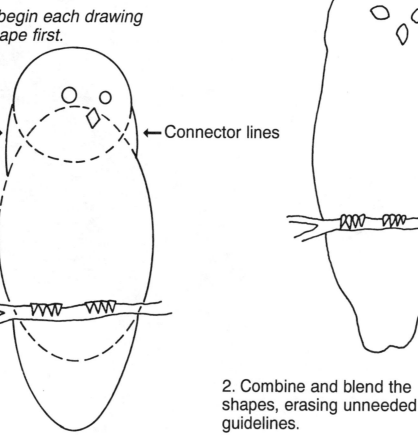

←Connector lines

1. Begin with a lightly drawn large oval for the owl's body. Add an overlapping circle for its head, and connect the two shapes. Add the other basic guideline shapes for the eyes, beak, tree limb, claws, and tail feathers.

2. Combine and blend the shapes, erasing unneeded guidelines.

3. Add details to the eyes and face, and define the tail feathers. Complete your spotted owl drawing by adding squiggly horizontal lines and shading.

Mediterranean Monk Seal

Flash fact: *There are probably fewer than 500 of these seals left in the world today.*

These shy seals breed inside caves on Mediterranean beaches. As more and more tourists visit the beaches, there are fewer spots for the seals. Pollution has also taken its toll.

1. Lightly draw a large oval for the seal's body and a smaller one for its head. Add the other basic guideline shapes for the eye, snout, and front and tail flippers. Connect the shapes as shown.

2. Blend the shapes into a sleek, smooth, seal body shape. Keep sketching and erasing until you are satisfied.

3. Complete the facial features and add lots of shading and texture to finish your monk seal drawing.

Cheetah

The cheetah—the fastest animal on land—
can run for short distances at the amazing speed
of over 60 miles per hour! Long, slender legs and a
streamlined body make it a perfect running machine.
Reduced habitat has resulted in endangered status
for this magnificent cat.

*Note: Draw these key steps carefully. By connecting the ovals,
you have created a solid foundation. This will give your figure a
more realistic look after you've completed the next steps.*

2. Add the basic shapes for the legs,
paws, and long, curved tail. If you're not
satisfied with any part of your drawing,
erase and start again.

1. Begin this cat by lightly drawing a circle for the
shoulder area and an oval for the rear flank.
Connect the shapes with two curved lines, forming
the back and belly. Then draw a smaller circle for
the head and connect it to the body. Sketch in the
ears, snout, and a small triangle for the eye.

Flash fact: The cheetah is the only cat that cannot pull in its claws.

3. Curve and blend all the parts together into a smooth body shape.

4. First, complete the cheetah's face. Add the nose, mouth, eye, and whiskers. Add all the other details and finish your drawing by covering the cheetah with its famous spots.

Black-footed Ferret

This very rare ferret's existence has long been tied to the survival of prairie dogs, on which they prey. Once widespread throughout the American Great Plains, prairie dog "towns" have been greatly reduced due to the spread of agriculture, ranching, and housing.

Note: It's usually easier to begin each drawing by sketching the largest shape first.

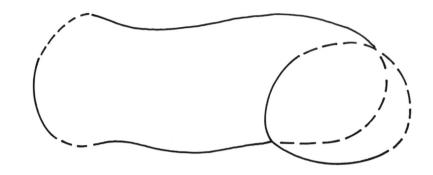

1. Start with a lightly drawn, long oval shape for the body. Add a smaller overlapping oval for the hindquarters.

2. Sketch a triangular shape for the head and connect it to the body. Then add the four short legs and paws, and the curly tail, as shown.

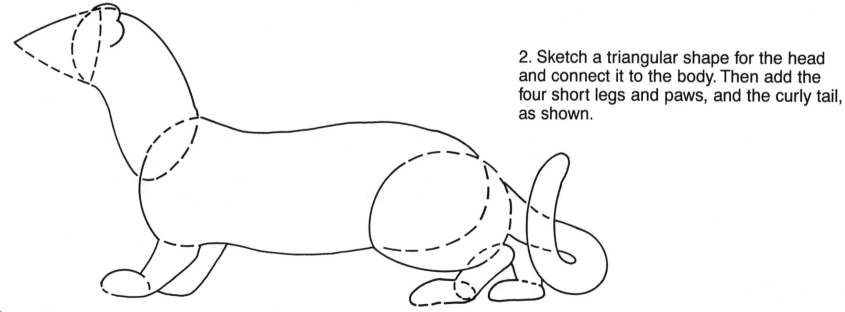

3. Start erasing any guidelines that are no longer needed as you combine the shapes together.

Remember: If you are not satisfied with the way any part of your drawing looks, erase it and start again. Practice Makes Perfect.

4. Finish the facial features and add details and shading to complete your drawing. Note the dark "mask" on the ferret's face.

Flash fact: In the 1950s, the tiny, two-pound black-footed ferret was considered extinct. Several colonies of them have been discovered since then. It is one of the rarest mammals in the world.

Hawaiian Goose

Hunted to the brink of extinction by humans and mongooses, only about 30 Hawaiian geese were still alive by the late 1940s. Captive breeding programs have increased their present numbers to about 500.

Remember to keep these lines lightly drawn.

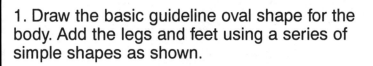

2. Add a small oval for the head, and an eye and beak. Connect the head to the body. Add the basic shape for the tail feathers.

1. Draw the basic guideline oval shape for the body. Add the legs and feet using a series of simple shapes as shown.

Flash fact: The Hawaiian goose is also known as "nene."

Once you've mastered drawing a variety of animals, use your imagination and create a scene including several of them in it.

3. Blend and refine the shapes into a smooth outline of the goose, erasing any guidelines you no longer need.

Keep erasing and drawing until you are satisfied with the way your outline looks.

4. Add overlapping square shapes for the body feathers and shade them in. Finish your drawing by adding details and additional patches of shading.

Humpback Whale

Humpback whales are baleen whales. They have no teeth. Instead, they have comblike filters, called baleen plates, attached to their upper jaws which are used to strain tiny plants and animals from the water.

1. Start with a large oval for the middle part of the body. Long curved lines form the head and lower body sections. Use triangular shapes for the front flippers and tailfins.

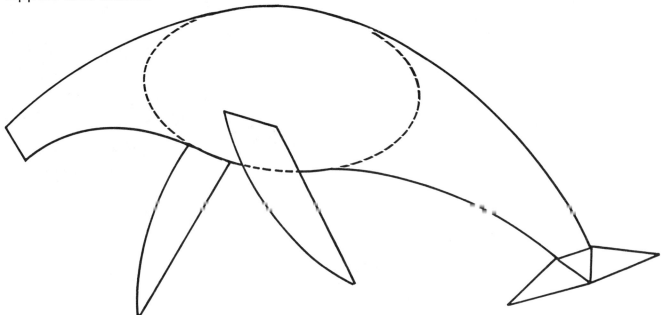

Flash fact: Humpback whales have been protected since 1946. Humpbacks bear only one calf every 2-3 years, limiting the possibility of greatly increasing their numbers.

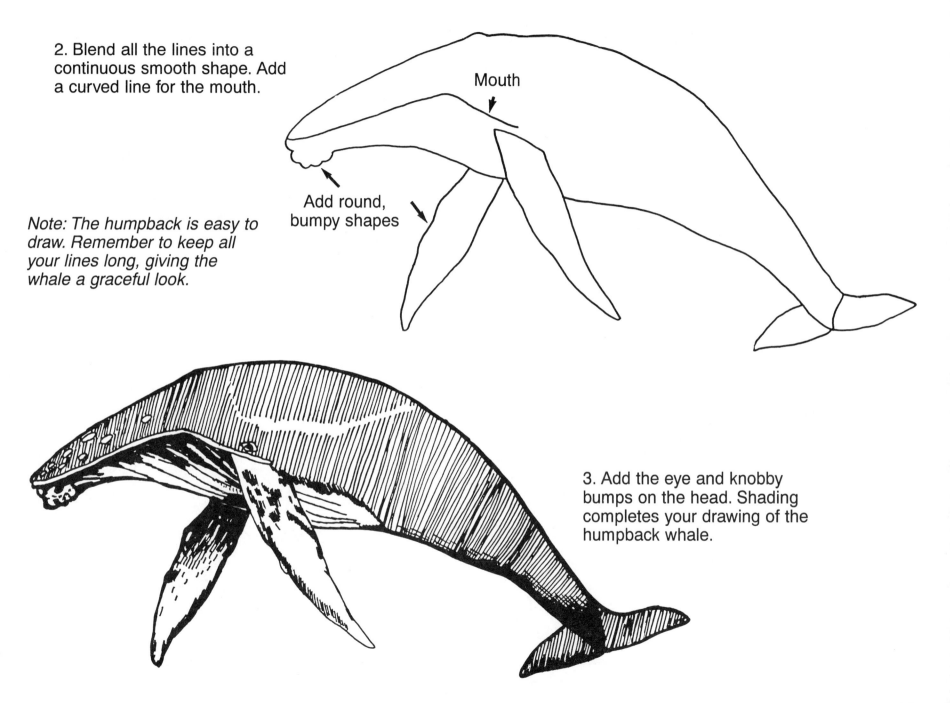

2. Blend all the lines into a continuous smooth shape. Add a curved line for the mouth.

Mouth

Add round, bumpy shapes

Note: The humpback is easy to draw. Remember to keep all your lines long, giving the whale a graceful look.

3. Add the eye and knobby bumps on the head. Shading completes your drawing of the humpback whale.

Fijian Banded Iguana

This rare, long-toed lizard likes to hang out in trees.
But trees on the Pacific islands where it lives are
becoming scarce, causing this iguana to become endangered.

*Note: It's usually easier to begin each drawing
by sketching the largest shape first.*

1. First, draw a long, free-form oval for the
iguana's body. Next, add two overlapping
ovals for the head. Remember to keep all
guideline shapes lightly drawn. You will
revise them later.

2. Sketch two very long lines to create the
curvy tail. Then add the other basic
shapes for the legs, feet, and long claws.

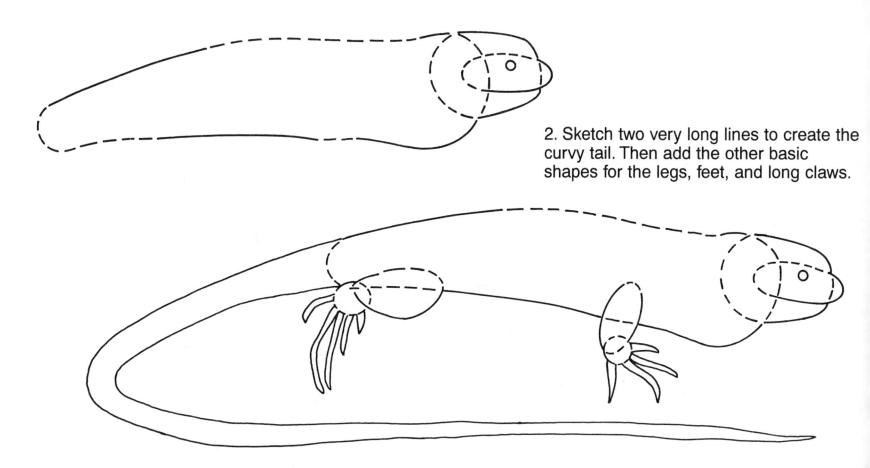

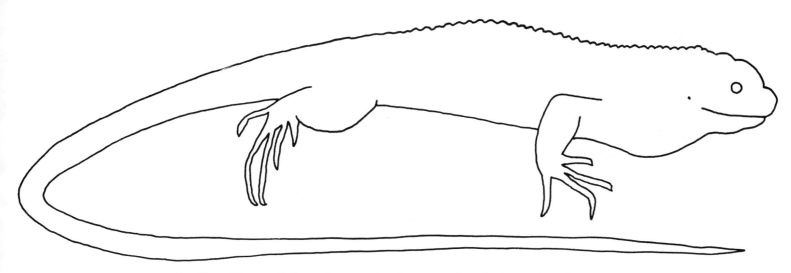

3. Combine all the shapes to form a simple line drawing.
Note the squiggly line on the iguana's back.

Flash fact: One of the iguana's worst enemies is the mongoose, which eats the iguana's eggs and young.

4. Finish your drawing by adding details and texture to the head and neck. If you wish to color your drawing, the shaded bands running all the way to the tip of the tail are dark green. The unshaded bands are light green.

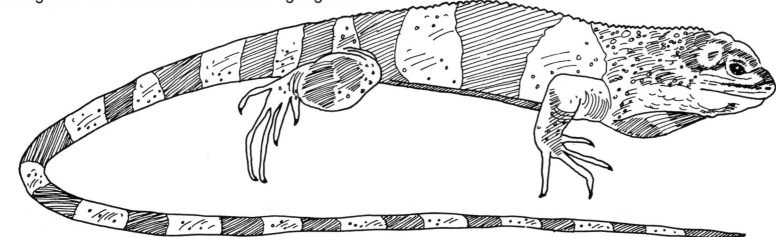

Giant Armadillo

The increasingly rare South American giant armadillo measures five feet from nose to tail. Except for its soft underside, the armadillo is covered with hard, bony plates which protect it from its enemies. The armadillo's long, sharp claws are ideal for digging after insects.

Note: Draw these key steps carefully. By connecting the basic guideline shapes, you have created a solid foundation. This will give your figure a more realistic look after you've completed the next steps.

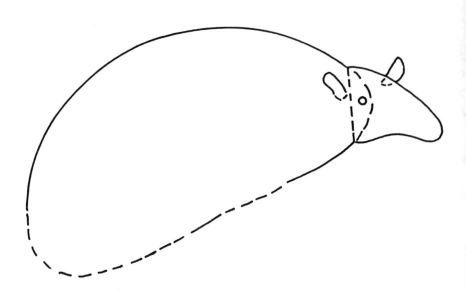

1. Draw a large free-form oval for the body and a triangular shape for the head. Add guideline shapes for the eye and ears.

2. Add a long tail, and feet and claws using simple guideline shapes. Note the huge claws. Draw a long, wavy line starting at the nose, across the whole body, and ending at the tail.

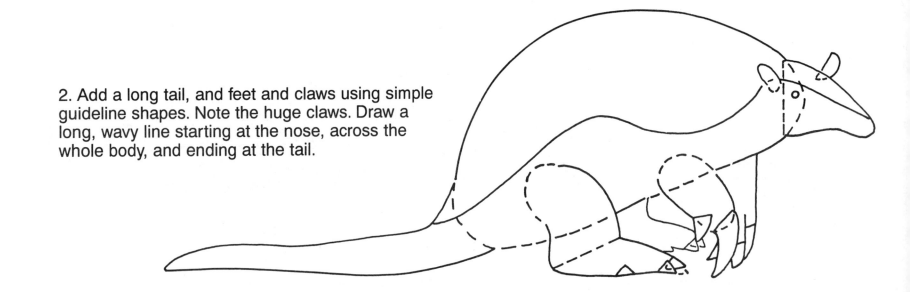

. Erase any guidelines you no longer need
s you blend all the shapes together into a
omplete body outline. Continue to refine all
ne lines and shapes until you're satisfied
/ith the way the armadillo looks.

*Flash fact: Despite its size and
rigid appearance, a giant armadillo,
using its thick tail for balance, can
stand on its two hind feet.*

4. Carefully add lots of scales, texture, and
shading to complete your picture. The more
time you spend on details, the more finished
your drawing will look.

Scimitar-Horned Oryx

This rarest of antelopes is found in Arabia and the semi-desert areas of the Sahara. By the mid-1980s, due to excessive hunting, this magnificent animal was on the brink of extinction.

1. Begin the oryx with two ovals, one for the shoulder area, and the other for the hindquarter. The connecting lines between the two ovals form the back and belly. Next, draw ovals and a circle for the head, and connect it to the body.

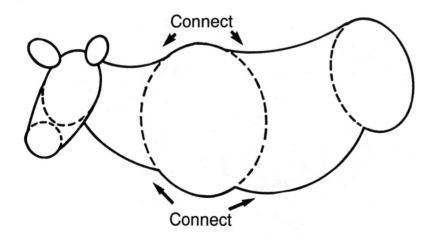

Connect

Connect

Taper

Triangles

2. Add more ovals for the top part of the legs and connect them to the triangular hooves. Add very long, curved horns and a tail.

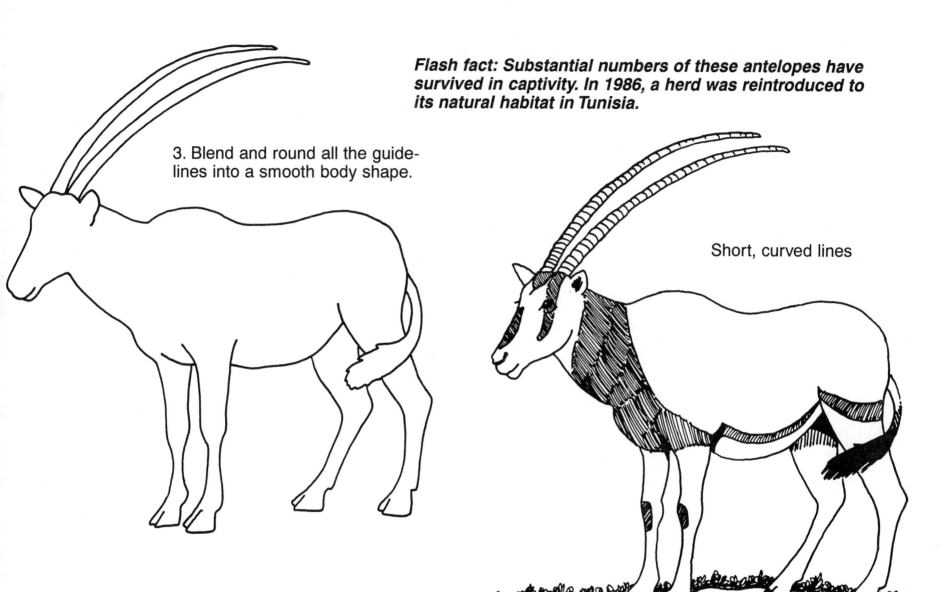

Flash fact: Substantial numbers of these antelopes have survived in captivity. In 1986, a herd was reintroduced to its natural habitat in Tunisia.

3. Blend and round all the guide-lines into a smooth body shape.

Short, curved lines

Always begin your drawings with the first step. Even though the finished drawing may appear difficult, you can draw it if you follow along, step by step.

4. Add the eye, nose, mouth, and hooves. Complete the oryx by adding texture to the horns, and shading the body as shown.

Helmeted Hornbill

This Southeast Asian bird is threatened by loss of habitat due to tree felling and poachers.

Note: It's usually easier to begin each drawing by sketching the largest shape first.

1. Start by drawing a free-form oval for the bird's body and a smaller one for its head. Connect the shapes with a curved neck line. Add the eye, the large triangular beak, and the crest on top of the beak.

2. Sketch in two long, overlapping ovals for the tail feathers. Add the additional basic shapes as shown. Always draw your guidelines lightly in steps 1 and 2—it will be easier to erase them later.

3. Blend the lines and shapes together, erasing unnecessary guidelines. Note that due to the feathers, the outline is not completely smooth.

4. Finish drawing the eye and crested beak. Then carefully add the body feathers by first sketching overlapping ovals and then shading them in. Don't forget to draw a branch for the hornbill to perch on.

Leatherback Sea Turtle

Overhunting and pollution have combined to reduce most sea turtle species to an endangered state. The leatherback is by far the largest of all turtles, on land or at sea. An adult can weigh 1,500 pounds and measure eight feet in length.

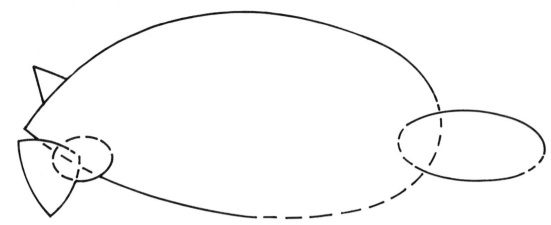

1. Begin by lightly sketching a large oval for the body and a smaller overlapping one for the head and neck. Add the guideline shapes for the back flippers.

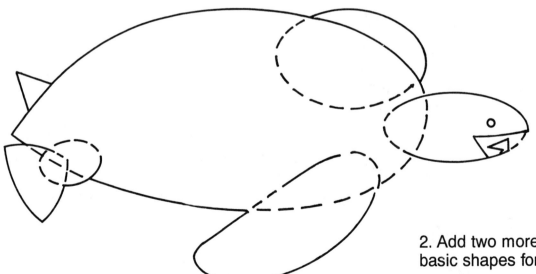

2. Add two more ovals for the front flippers, and the basic shapes for the eye, beak, and mouth.

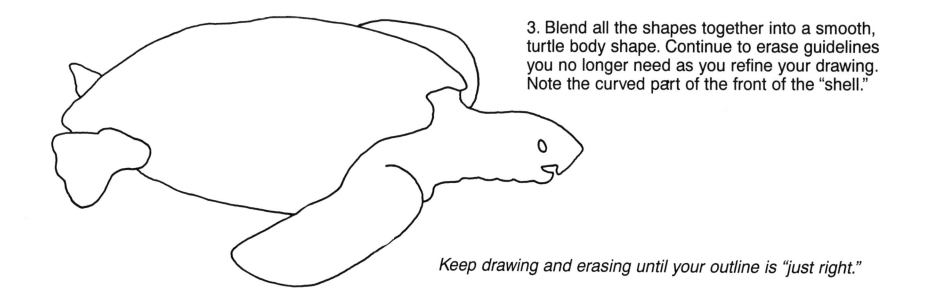

3. Blend all the shapes together into a smooth, turtle body shape. Continue to erase guidelines you no longer need as you refine your drawing. Note the curved part of the front of the "shell."

Keep drawing and erasing until your outline is "just right."

Flash fact: The leatherback sea turtle is the only sea turtle without a true shell. Instead, it's covered with tough, leathery skin.

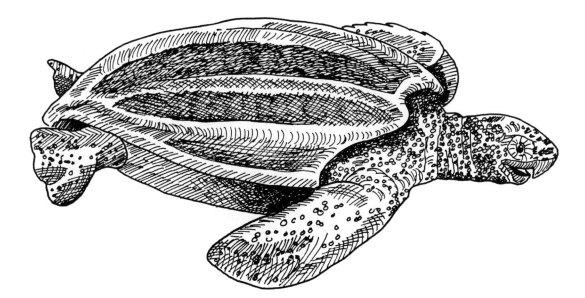

4. Complete your drawing by adding lots of different textures and shading.

Aye-Aye

The aye-aye and other lemurs are only found on the island of Madagascar. This pop-eyed creature has a super-long middle finger, which it uses to pull insects out of tree bark.

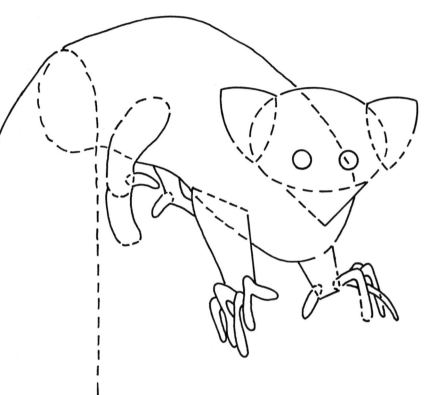

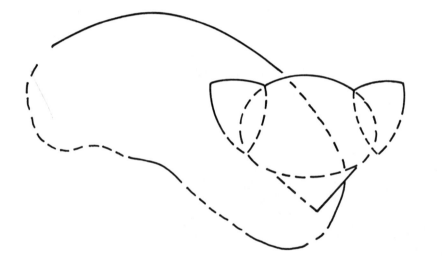

1. Draw the basic guideline shape for the body. Then add the overlapping oval for the head and the triangular shapes for the ears and snout.

2. Add the long oval shape for the tail and two circles for the eyes. Then carefully create the legs and fingers.

Flash fact: Local people believe that the harmless aye-aye brings bad luck. For this reason they are often needlessly killed.

3. Erase unnecessary guidelines as you blend the shapes together. Carefully curve all the body lines into a smooth outline.

4. Add the nose and mouth, and complete the eyes. Then add heavy shading and the other finishing touches. When you're done, add a tree branch for the aye-aye to walk on.

Indri

Indris belong to the lemur family. They only live on preserves set up to protect them on the island of Madagascar. Loss of their forest habitat has reduced the already small numbers of indris.

1. Start with large ovals for the indri's body and leg. Add the foot and front paw, and connect the paw to the body. Next, draw circles for the head and ears.

Connect

2. Draw a triangle for the snout and two small circles for the eyes. Add a long, rectangular shape for the tree section on which the indri is sitting, and additional lines as shown.

Add

Flash fact: Although some indris are protected in preserves, a human population explosion in Madagascar has led to greater loss of the indri's true home, the forest.

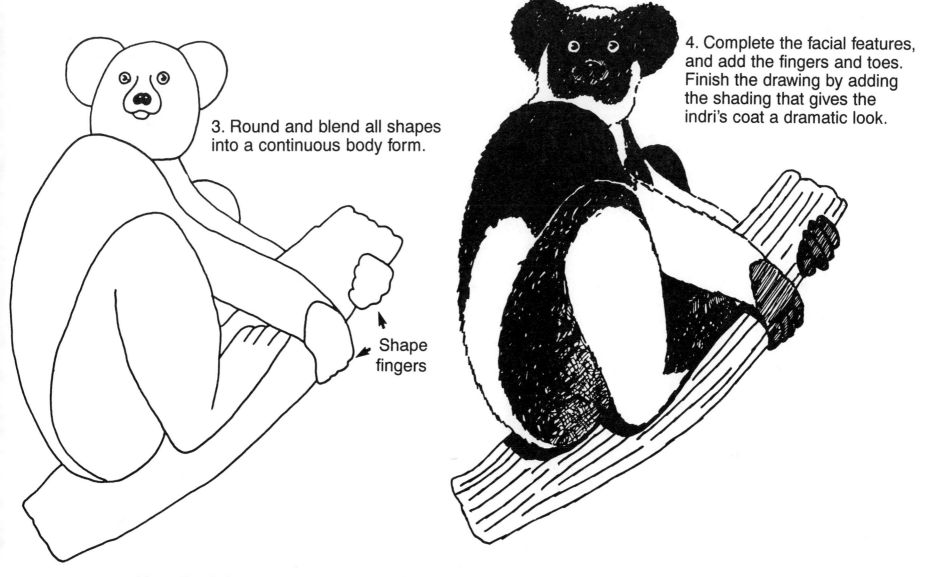

3. Round and blend all shapes into a continuous body form.

Shape fingers

4. Complete the facial features, and add the fingers and toes. Finish the drawing by adding the shading that gives the indri's coat a dramatic look.

Note: Don't forget to erase unnecessary guidelines.

Chimpanzee

Chimpanzees live in western and central Africa. They have disappeared from many areas as their habitat is destroyed. They are also illegally captured and sold for medical experiments.

Note: Draw these key steps carefully. By connecting the ovals, you have created a solid foundation. This will give your figure a more realistic look after you've completed the next steps.

2. Draw guidelines for the chimp's arms, hands, and feet. Then add the shapes for the eyes, nose, and mouth. Remember to erase any unnecessary lines as you continue to refine your drawing.

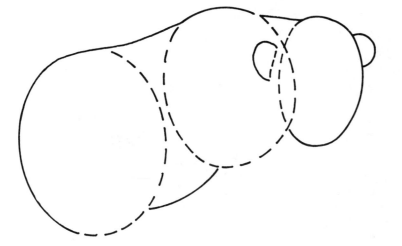

1. Start with the three basic oval guideline shapes. Note the overlapping head and shoulder ovals. Connect the ovals and add the ears.

Flash fact: Chimps are one of the very few animals besides humans to use tools. They use sticks to dig for insects and stones to crack open shells.

3. Blend the shapes into a smooth body outline. Keep erasing and drawing until you're satisfied with the way your drawing looks. Remember: Practice Makes Perfect.

4. Complete the facial features and define the fingers and toes. Add the heavy shading with a black felt-tip pen.

Indigo Macaw

So many South American macaws have been trapped and sold as pets that they have completely disappeared from many areas. The purplish-blue indigo, at a length of up to three feet, is the longest of all parrots.

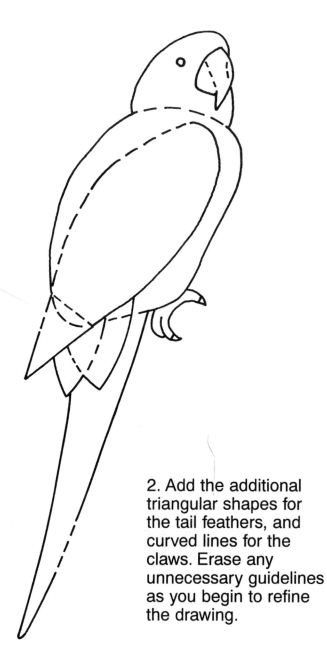

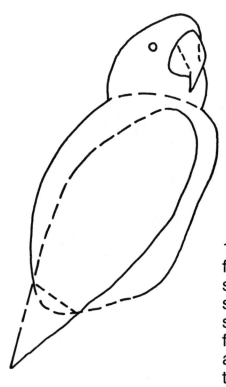

1. Carefully draw the basic free-form oval guideline shape for the body. Then sketch a smaller oval shape within the first one for the wing, adding a triangle at the lower tip. Add the other guideline shapes for the head.

2. Add the additional triangular shapes for the tail feathers, and curved lines for the claws. Erase any unnecessary guidelines as you begin to refine the drawing.

Flash fact: Although trapping macaws is illegal in most places, some birds are still smuggled out. An indigo macaw can sell for well over $5,000 in a pet store.

3. Blend and smooth all the shapes together into a complete body outline.

4. Define the individual feathers before shading them in. Add details, texture, and more shading to give your drawing a realistic look. Don't forget to draw a limb for the macaw to perch on.

Jaguar

Hunted for years for its beautiful coat, jaguars are now a protected species. Due to the ever-shrinking forests of Central and South America, the number of jaguars is decreasing with each passing year.

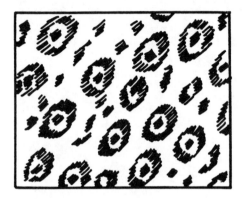

Unlike other spotted cats, the jaguar's spots are enclosed by a circular pattern.

1. Begin with a series of lightly drawn, interconnecting ovals as shown.

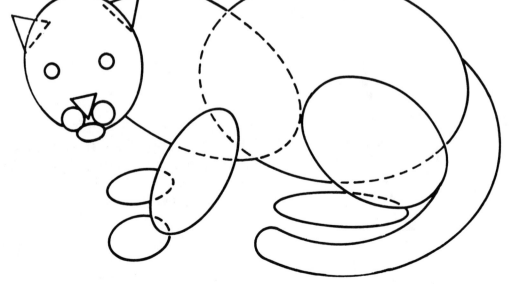

2. Add guidelines for the ears, eyes, nose, and mouth. Add additional ovals for the legs and paws, and long, curved lines for the tail.

Indent

Indent

3. Connect and blend all the shapes together. Erase the guidelines you no longer need.

Flash fact: As South American forests in Brazil and Peru are chopped down, jaguars have no place to go. Hunters also seek the large cat's beautiful skin. Reserves and anti-hunting laws now protect these sleek animals.

4. For the final step, add in all the details. Draw the jaguar's unique coat pattern and some background scenery. Use your imagination and create a jungle scene.

Resplendent Quetzal

This beautiful Central American bird has a red breast and green tail feathers that extend up to 30 inches. Unfortunately, this beauty makes people want to keep them as pets, and they are fast disappearing from the wild.

Note: Always draw your guidelines lightly in steps 1 and 2—it will be easier to erase them later.

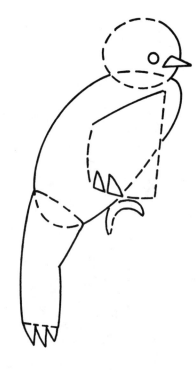

1. Begin with an oval for the body and an overlapping circle for the head. Add the other guideline shapes for the wing, foot, and upper tail feathers.

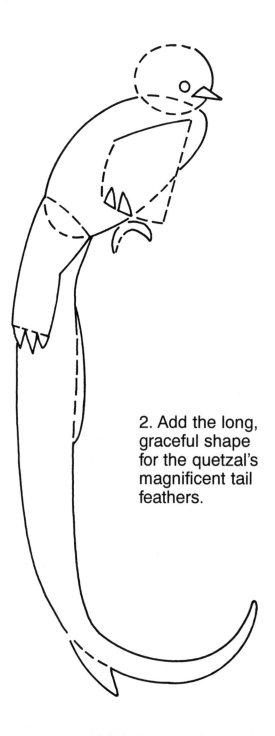

2. Add the long, graceful shape for the quetzal's magnificent tail feathers.

Flash fact: Much of the mountain forest that the quetzal lives in is being cleared to make way for farming.

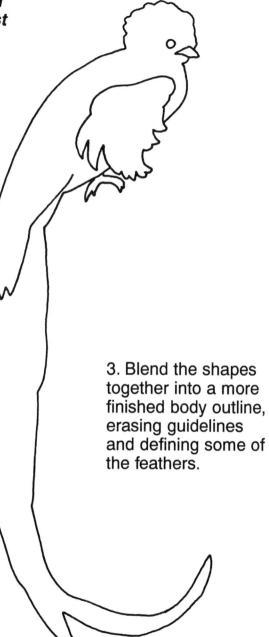

3. Blend the shapes together into a more finished body outline, erasing guidelines and defining some of the feathers.

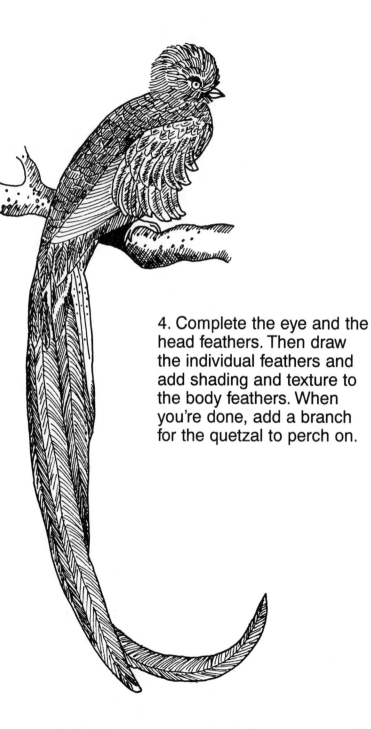

4. Complete the eye and the head feathers. Then draw the individual feathers and add shading and texture to the body feathers. When you're done, add a branch for the quetzal to perch on.

Spectacled Bear

Note: It's usually easier to begin each drawing by sketching the largest shape first.

This bear gets its name from the white rings around its eyes. It lives in trees, hunting for fruit at night and sleeping by day. It is becoming increasingly scarce as its natural habitat is cleared for farmland.

1. Begin with a large rectangular shape for the bear's body. Add an overlapping circle for its head, and the other basic guideline shapes as shown.

2. Add the guideline shapes for the arms, paws, legs, and feet. Remember to keep these lines lightly drawn.

Flash fact: The spectacled bear is the only bear that lives in South America.

3. Blend the shapes together into an outline drawing of the bear. Add claws to the paws and feet.

4. Add details and shading to this furry creature. Be careful when shading the face. The white area around the bear's eyes makes it seem as if it's wearing "spectacles."

Black Rhinoceros

The black rhinoceros can be found in the grassland, bush, and forest areas of Africa.

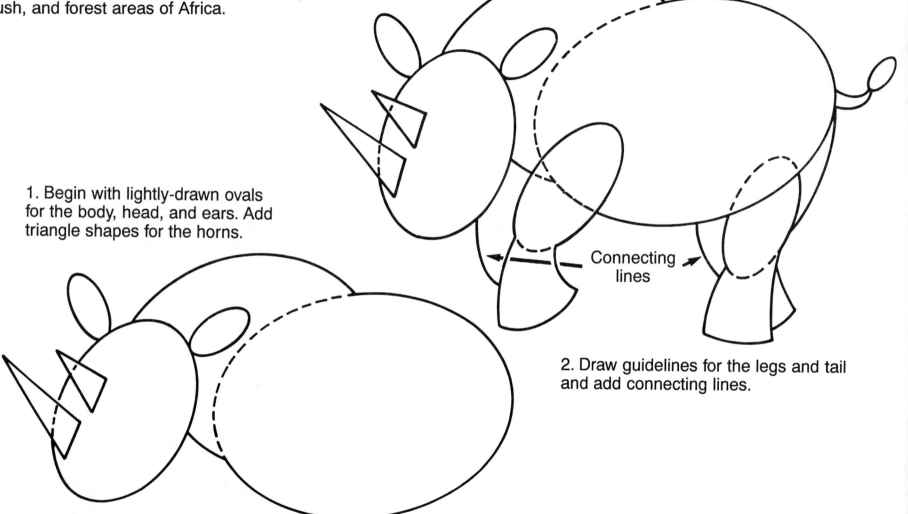

1. Begin with lightly-drawn ovals for the body, head, and ears. Add triangle shapes for the horns.

Connecting lines

2. Draw guidelines for the legs and tail and add connecting lines.

Note: It's easier to draw the largest shape first, then the smaller ones.

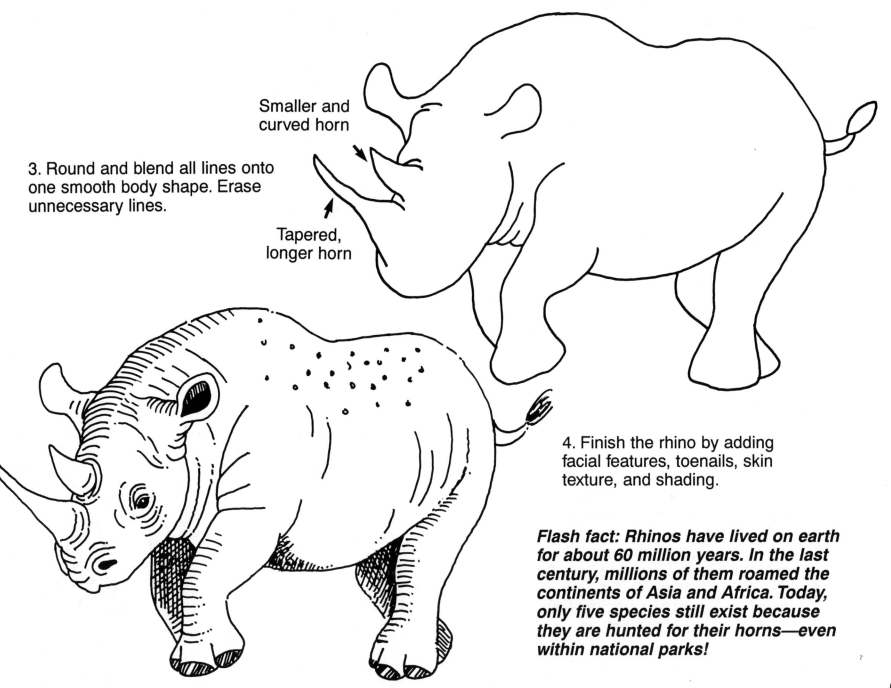

Smaller and
curved horn

3. Round and blend all lines onto
one smooth body shape. Erase
unnecessary lines.

Tapered,
longer horn

4. Finish the rhino by adding
facial features, toenails, skin
texture, and shading.

*Flash fact: Rhinos have lived on earth
for about 60 million years. In the last
century, millions of them roamed the
continents of Asia and Africa. Today,
only five species still exist because
they are hunted for their horns—even
within national parks!*

Queen Alexandra's Birdwing

Found only in New Guinea, this is the biggest butterfly in the world. It has been hunted because of its great value to collectors. Some people are now planning to breed the birdwing on ranches.

2. Lightly sketch four overlapping ovals for the wings.

1. Start this beautiful butterfly by lightly sketching two slender overlapping oval guideline shapes for the body. Add two tiny circles for the eyes and two graceful lines for the antennae.

Flash fact: This butterfly's wingspan is between six and ten inches. A real one would barely fit on this page.

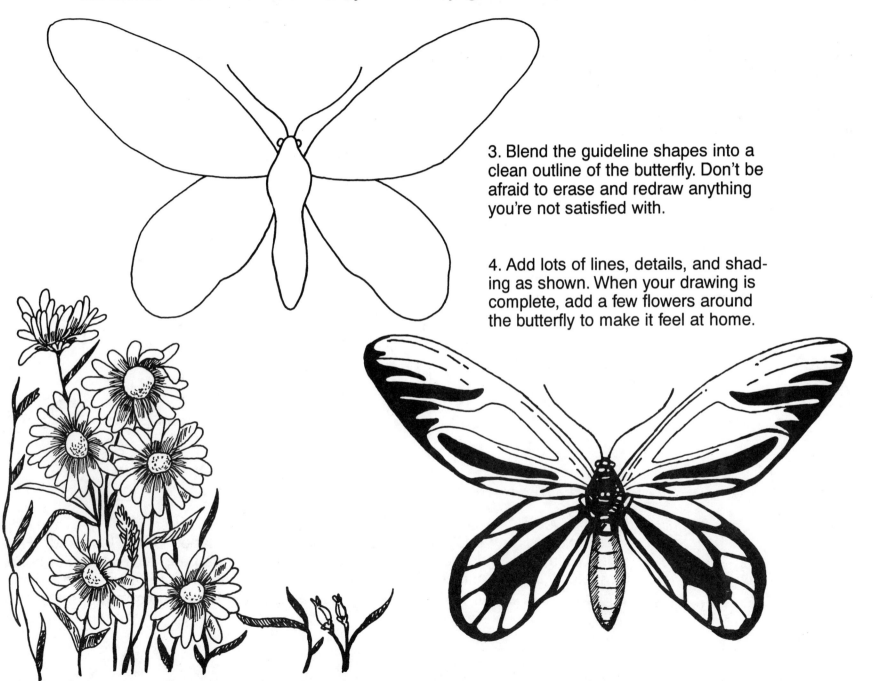

3. Blend the guideline shapes into a clean outline of the butterfly. Don't be afraid to erase and redraw anything you're not satisfied with.

4. Add lots of lines, details, and shading as shown. When your drawing is complete, add a few flowers around the butterfly to make it feel at home.

Przewalski's Horse

This endangered animal is named after the Polish explorer who discovered it in the late 1800s. Once abundant throughout central Asia, this wild horse has been hunted by man to near extinction.

Remember to draw these guidelines lightly. They will be easier to erase as you refine and complete your picture.

1. Start with a thick free-form oval for the body. Add two smaller overlapping ones for the shoulder and rump.

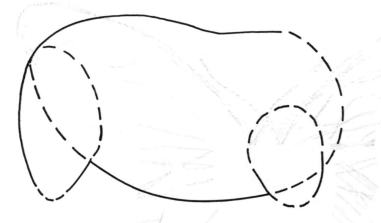

2. Continue adding basic guideline shapes for the legs and hooves. Then draw an oval for the head and a circle for the nose, and connect the two shapes. Add the ears and connect the head to the body. Finally, add a guideline for the horse's mane.

3. Blend the shapes into a smooth outline sketch, erasing any guidelines you no longer need.

Flash fact: Within a few hours after birth, a wild colt can run fast enough to keep up with the herd.

4. Define the hooves and add details to the horse's face. Draw short, straight lines for the tough, stubby mane. Add shading to complete your picture.

Shortnose Sturgeon

Sturgeons live in the open sea most of the time. They swim inland through rivers and streams only to lay their eggs. With more and more dams being built, it becomes harder each year for the fish to get through.

Remember: All lines in steps 1 and 2 should be lightly drawn.

1. Sketch a very long oval, rounded at the front end and pointed at the back end, for the body. Add the head and pointy snout, and triangular shapes for the tail.

2. Add the eye and fins, and a row of small diamond shapes along the length of the sturgeon's body.

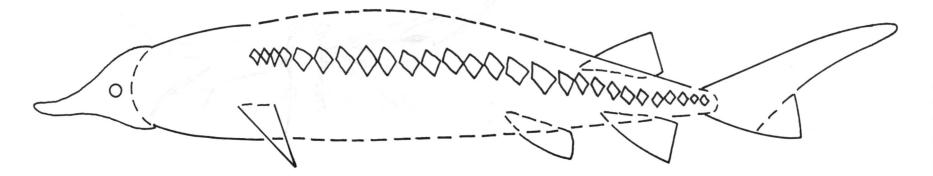

Flash fact: Sturgeon have been overhunted for food. In addition, females contain one of the world's expensive delicacies—caviar, made from her eggs.

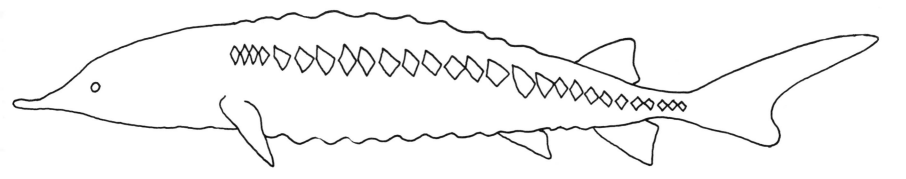

3. Blend the shapes together to form a simple line drawing. Note that the outlines of the back and belly are bumpy, not straight.

4. Lots of different textures and shading are required to complete this picture. First, add the details. Then get to work on the shading until your picture is finished.

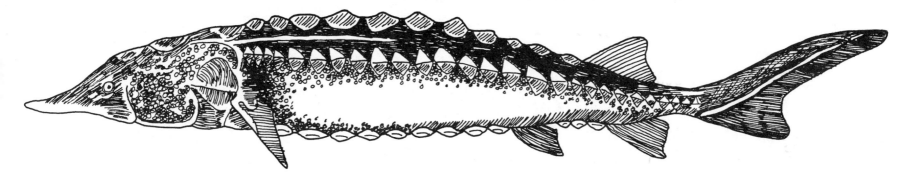

Giant Otter

Giant otters live in family groups on the banks of several rivers in South America. They can measure over six feet in length and 75 pounds in weight. This increasingly rare otter is threatened by overhunting and loss of habitat.

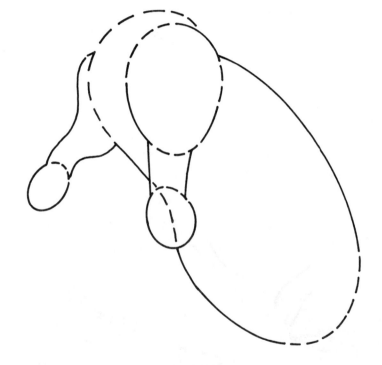

1. Begin with a large oval for the body. Draw another oval for the shoulder and one for the left paw, and connect them. Then draw the right paw and connect it to the body.

2. Draw an oval guideline for the otter's head and connect it to the body. Add the nose, eye, and ear. Then add guideline shapes for the rear legs and paws, and the long, curving tail.

*Flash fact:
Otters make
many different
sounds—they
chirp, chatter,
bark, and growl.*

4. Add the mouth and refine the facial features. Add shading, details, and the finishing touches, like whiskers, to give your otter drawing a realistic look.

. Blend the lines and shapes together, rasing guidelines as you go along. he basic otter body shape is now omplete.

Jote: Make sure that you are satisfied vith the way your drawing looks before oing to step 4.

75

Ivory Billed Woodpecker

This black and white woodpecker eats beetle grubs found only in the dead wood of very old trees. Logging has destroyed many first-growth forests, and the woodpecker's food along with them.

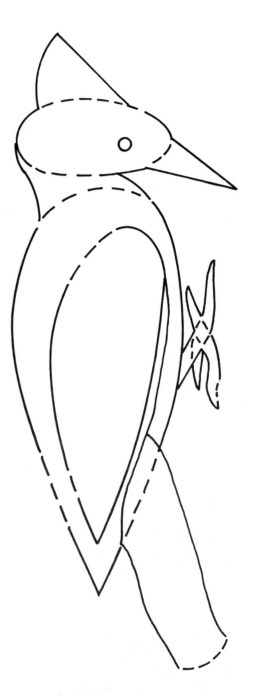

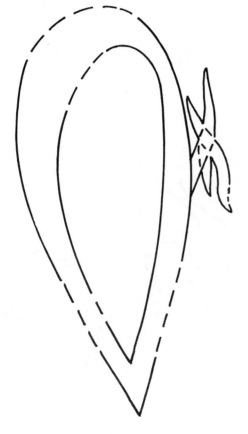

1. Start by drawing a large oval— pointed at the bottom end—for the body. Then draw a similar oval inside the first one for the wing. Note how the top of the wing oval is pointed in a different direction from the body. Add the simple shapes for the foot.

2. Add an oval for the head and connect it to the body. Then add the other basic shapes for the eye, crest, beak, and tail feathers.

3. Blend the shapes together into a smooth woodpecker body outline.

Keep erasing and sketching until you are satisfied with the way your drawing looks before going to step 4.

4. Define the tail and wing feathers before shading them in. Then add lots of details and texture. Create the (red) crest on the bird's head with short, slightly bent lines. Finally, add a tree for the woodpecker to peck into.

Rodrigues Flying Fox

This rare, fruit-eating bat lives on Rodrigues Island in the Indian Ocean.

Note: Keep all your guidelines lightly drawn. They will be easier to erase later on.

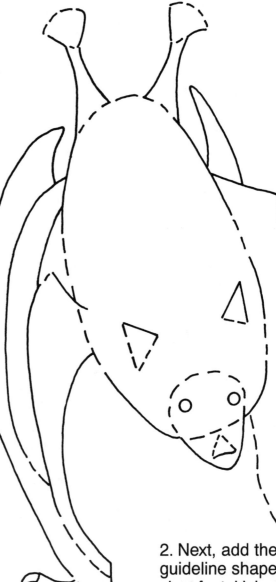

1. Begin your drawing with a large oval for the bat's body. Add two small triangles for the ears and an overlapping free-form oval for the head. Then, add two small circles for the eyes and another small triangle for the nose.

2. Next, add the legs and guideline shapes for the claw feet. Using a series of simple lines and shapes, add the wings.

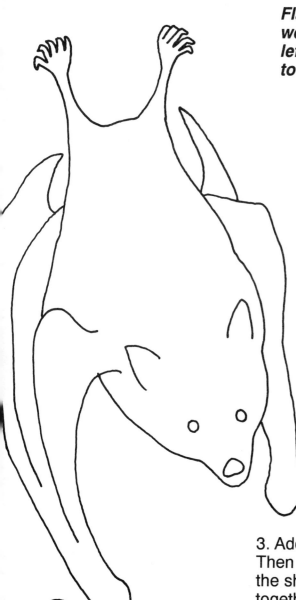

Flash fact: In the 1970s there were less than 80 of these bats left. Today, numbers have risen to about 400.

Before going to the next step, make sure that you are satisfied with the way your drawing looks so far.

3. Add the toes to the feet. Then combine and blend all the shapes and lines together into a smooth outline of the bat. Erase any unnecessary guidelines as you go along.

4. Add the final details to the bat's face and all the finishing touches. Use lots of shading, as shown, to complete your drawing.

Snow Leopard

Living high in the mountains of central Asia, the snow leopard is still hunted for its beautiful, valuable fur.

1. Begin by lightly sketching two large, overlapping ovals for the body. Then add guideline shapes for the head, ears, and mouth.

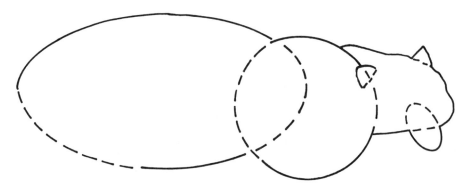

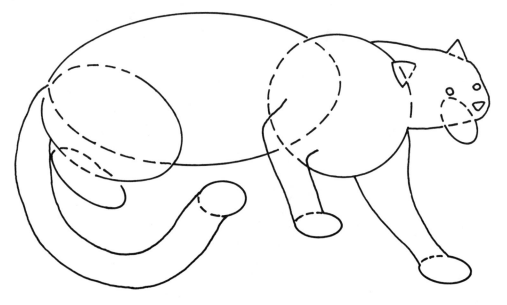

2. Add the additional basic guideline shapes for the legs and feet. Then add the eyes, nose, and the long, curved tail.

Note: This is a very important step. It establishes the basic overall structure and look of your drawing. In steps 3 and 4, you are simply refining and adding details to the figure you have created in steps 1 and 2.

3. Blend the shapes together, erasing any guidelines you no longer need as you go along. Keep refining your picture until you're satisfied with the way it looks.

Flash fact: It is estimated that between 4,000 and 5,000 snow leopards still survive in remote areas of Afghanistan, Siberia, and Tibet.

4. Add all the details to the face and mouth. Then carefully add the leopard's spots. When you're satisfied with your work, add a shadow beneath the leopard to give your drawing a dramatic look.

A Indian Python

This
natu

Ren

The Indian python can grow to over 20 feet. Its coils are powerful enough to squeeze a leopard to death. The python has suffered from loss of habitat, being hunted for its beautiful skin, and capture for the pet trade.

There are many overlapping shapes to draw in the first two steps, so proceed lightly and carefully. Remember: It's easy to draw any animal if you break it down into simple shapes first.

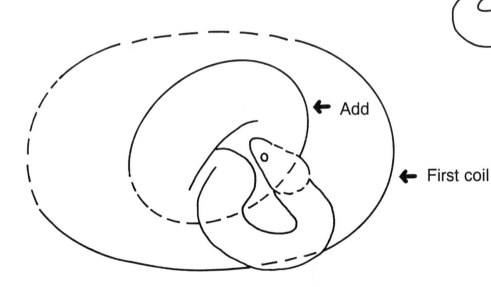

← Add

← First coil

Second coil
↓
Add
↓

← Add

1. Lightly draw a large oval shape. Add a smaller oval inside the first one. This part of the python's body is coiled around its prey. Draw the head, and using two curved lines, connect it to the center of the smaller oval.

2. Next, draw the long curved tail. Then, add another oval shape to form the second coil. This is a bit complicated so proceed slowly.

3. Blend and shape all the body lines together. Carefully erase the guidelines you no longer need. It helps to imagine what a pile of thick rope might look like.

Make sure you're satisfied with the way your picture looks before going to step 4.

4. Now, here's the fun part. Finish your drawing by adding texture, patterns, and shading. What do you think the python is coiled around?

Flash fact: The female Indian python is the snake that helps her eggs hatch. By coiling and vibrating her body around them, she keeps the eggs warm and speeds up the hatching.

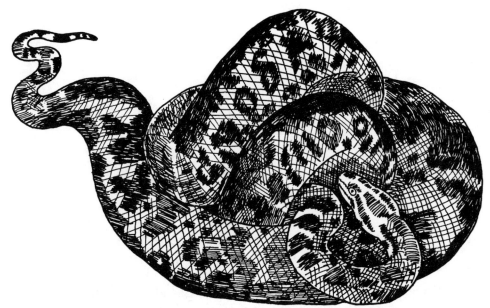

85

Proboscis Monkey

This strange-looking monkey has a large fleshy nose. It lives in riverside swamps and forests in Borneo. Much of its habitat has been cleared to make way for human settlement.

There are many overlapping shapes to draw in the first two steps, so proceed lightly and carefully until you've drawn the basic body structure.

2. Add the eyes, and complete the guideline shap for the rest of the arms, hands, legs, and feet.

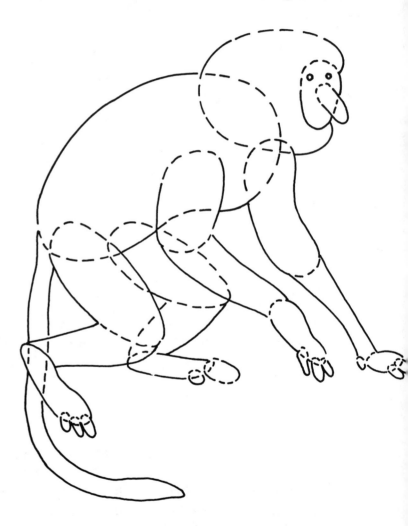

1. Begin with a large free-form oval guideline shape for the body and another one for the monkey's head. Within that oval draw two smaller ones for the face and big nose. Add the over-lapping oval guidelines for the upper arms and legs.

When you're completely satisfied with the way your drawing looks, begin adding the finishing touches.

4. Complete the facial features. Then add shading and other details to the mane and body. This monkey has long hair on its neck and chest and shorter hair on the rest of its body. Don't forget to add a little shading to that long nose!

3. Carefully erase any guidelines that you no longer need as you blend and refine the shapes and lines.

Flash fact: Only the male proboscis monkeys have a big nose. Sometimes they have to push their nose out of the way to eat!

Hawksbill Sea Turtle

Most marine turtles are at risk due to several reasons. They all lay their eggs on beaches, many of which are no longer deserted. They are also hunted for their meat in some areas of the world. Pollution has also taken its toll.

2. Add oval shapes and connector lines for the front flippers as shown.

← Connector line

Connector lines

1. Sketch a large oval that is pointed on one end for the body. Draw a small oval for the head, adding the eye and beak. Add the basic guideline shapes for the back flippers.

Flash fact: The hawksbill sea turtle's beautiful shell has been used to make jewelry and ornaments.

4. Divide the shell into sections, as shown, before adding lots of textures and shading for the finishing touches.

3. Blend and shape all the forms together, paying close attention to how all the shapes and lines interconnect. When you're satisfied with the way your sea turtle outline looks, start adding details. Note the jagged edges on the outline of the shell.

Brindled Wallaby

This small Australian creature is related to the kangaroo. It hops along, sometimes with a baby in its pouch, steadying itself with its long tail. The wallaby hops in a weird way; it whirls its arms around in circles as it jumps.

Note: Keep all your guidelines lightly drawn.
They will be easier to erase later on.

1. Draw the large, egg-shaped oval for the body in the direction as shown. Then add the other oval shapes for the head, eyes, nose, and right shoulder. Sketch in curved lines for the arms and tiny triangles for the claws.

2. Create the legs and feet with rectangles and triangular guideline shapes. Then add the long, curved tail.

Make sure you have built a solid foundation with the first two steps before continuing.

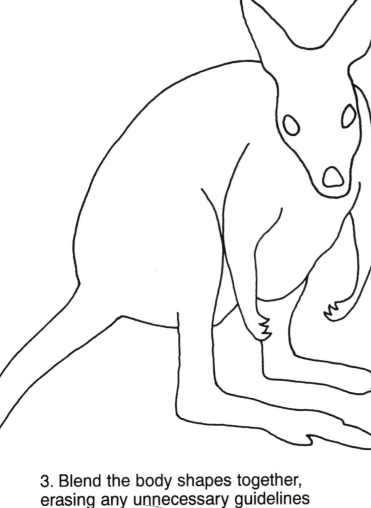

Flash fact: Once widespread, the brindled wallaby is now endangered due to sheep and cattle grazing on its grassy shrubland habitat.

3. Blend the body shapes together, erasing any unnecessary guidelines as you go along. Don't forget to indent the cheek lines.

4. Complete the eyes and nose, and add whiskers. Finish your wallaby drawing by adding details and lots of shading.

Vicuna

This South American relative of the camel numbered in the millions a few hundred years ago. Due to its valuable fur, only several thousand remained by the 1960s.

Remember: Keep all your guidelines lightly drawn, so that they may be easily erased later on.

1. Draw the large oval for the body and the smaller one for the head. Connect the two ovals. Then add guidelines for the ears, eye, and snout.

2. Add the additional guidelines for the legs, hooves, and tail.

Keep erasing and drawing until you are satisfied with the way your drawing looks.

3. Blend the lines and shapes together, erasing any unnecessary guidelines as you go along.

4. Complete the nose and mouth, and when you're satisfied with the way the vicuna looks, add shading for the finishing touch.

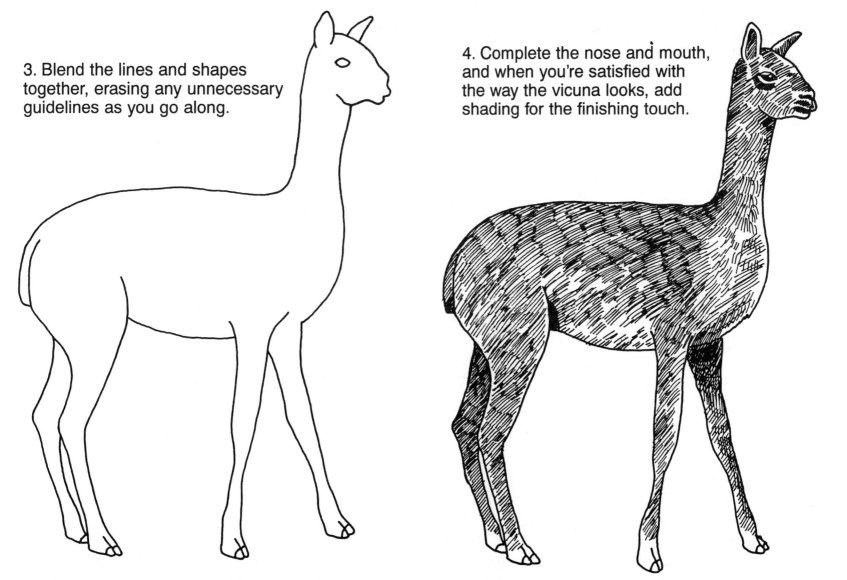

Flash fact: Conservation efforts have worked well for the vicuna. Careful protection has raised their numbers to over 90,000.

Dalmatian Pelican

Remember: All lines in steps 1 and 2 should always be lightly drawn. They will be erased or changed as you continue to create your picture.

This big, white seabird flies over the water looking for its dinner. As it plunges down, its lower bill expands to form a huge scoop for skimming fish out of the water.

Note: It's usually easier to begin each drawing by sketching the largest shape first.

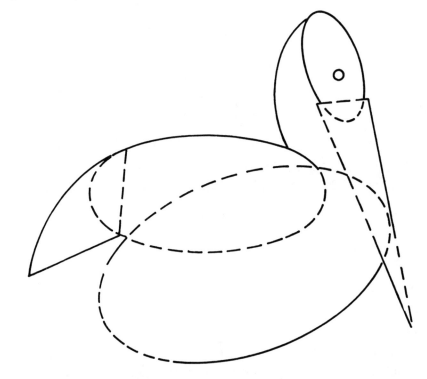

1. Begin with a large oval for the body. Add a smaller one for the overlapping wing and attach a triangular shape on the end. Draw a small oval for the head and a long triangle for the beak. Attach the head to the body with a single line.

2. Add two more triangles for the tail feathers and the other shapes for the legs and feet.

Flash fact: This bird's population has been drastically reduced as its marshy habitats have been drained and built over.

3. Blend the shapes together, erasing any unnecessary guidelines. Draw a long line down the center of the beak. Note the curved tip. The outline for the tail and wing feathers should be irregular.

4. When you're satisfied with the way the pelican looks, start adding details. Pay special attention to the overlapping wing feathers. Finally, add shading to complete the drawing.

California Condor

The California condor is extinct in the wild. Listed as endangered since 1967, a valiant effort has been made to breed these extraordinary birds in captivity and reintroduce them to their natural habitat.

With a wingspan of over 10 feet, condors can soar effortlessly for hours. They are the largest birds in North America.

1. Start with a narrow oval guideline for the body. Add a small oval for the head, and a curved, triangular shape for the tail. Connect long, curved lines to the body to form the wings and a series of triangles at the end of each wing for feathers.

Connect

Connect

Add triangle

2. Blend all the shapes into one body outline. Erase any guidelines you don't need.

Wavy line

Add ey

Complet beak

3. Complete the condor by drawing lots of short lines with curved edges to define the body and tail feathers.

Flash fact: California condors flourished a century ago when vast cattle ranches offered a regular food supply.

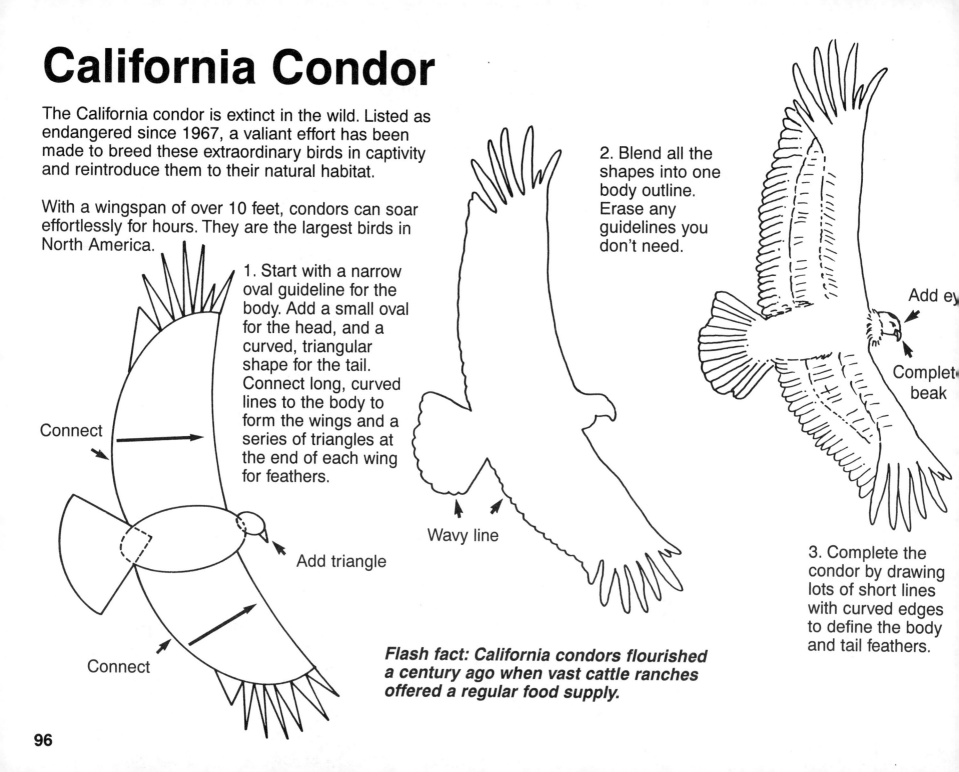

Galapagos Tortoise

This giant tortoise exists only on the Galapagos Islands, off the coast of South America. It can grow up to four feet in shell length and weigh 500 pounds or more. The Galapagos tortoise can live up to 200 years—longer than any other animal.

Flash fact: Galapagos tortoises are now very rare due to overhunting and loss of habitat. In addition, the tortoise's eggs are often eaten or destroyed by other animals.

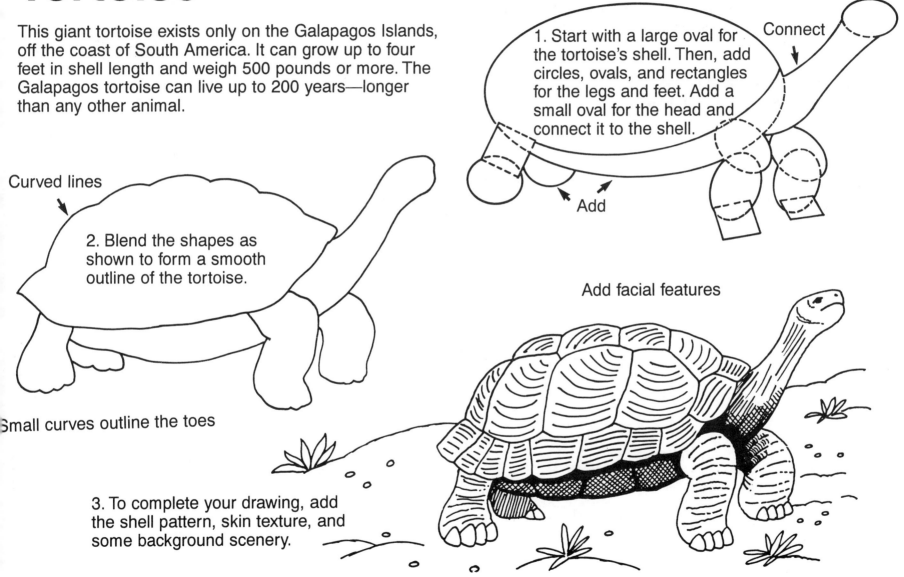

1. Start with a large oval for the tortoise's shell. Then, add circles, ovals, and rectangles for the legs and feet. Add a small oval for the head and connect it to the shell.

Connect

Add

Curved lines

2. Blend the shapes as shown to form a smooth outline of the tortoise.

Small curves outline the toes

Add facial features

3. To complete your drawing, add the shell pattern, skin texture, and some background scenery.

African Wild Dog

These wild dogs live in packs of up to 30 members and hunt as teams. They have great endurance and will chase their prey until it's exhausted. Many have been killed by farmers who are concerned for their livestock.

Note: It's usually easier to begin each drawing by sketching the largest shape first.

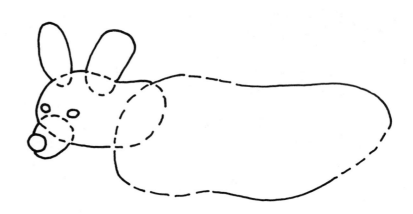

1. Begin with a large, free-form oval guideline shape for the body. Add a smaller overlapping oval for the head and neck. Then, using simple guideline shapes, sketch in the eyes, ears, snout, and nose.

2. Add the long legs and paws, and a pointy tail.

Keep erasing and drawing until you're completely satisfied with your work. Remember, practice makes perfect.

3. Combine and blend all the shapes and lines together into a smooth outline of the wild dog. Erase any guidelines you no longer need.

Flash fact: Once common throughout Africa south of the Sahara Desert, today they can mainly be found scattered about in a few national parks.

4. Add shading and irregular patches of darker color. No two African wild dogs are exactly the same color. They can be black, gray, or brown, or any shade in-between, and usually have blotches of white, orange, or yellow on their coats.

Tuatara

Once mistaken for a lizard, the tuatara is the only remaining member of an entire group of ancient reptiles. The Maori people of New Zealand gave the tuatara its name, which means "peaks on the back."

1. Begin with a large, free-form oval for the body. Add two overlapping ovals for the head and connect the top one to the body.

2. Add the long reptilian tail and sketch the guideline shapes for the feet and claws. Then, starting on the head, draw a line of small triangles all the way to the tip of the tail.

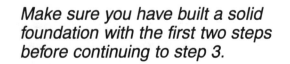

Make sure you have built a solid foundation with the first two steps before continuing to step 3.

Flash fact: Tuataras have been known to live for over 100 years.

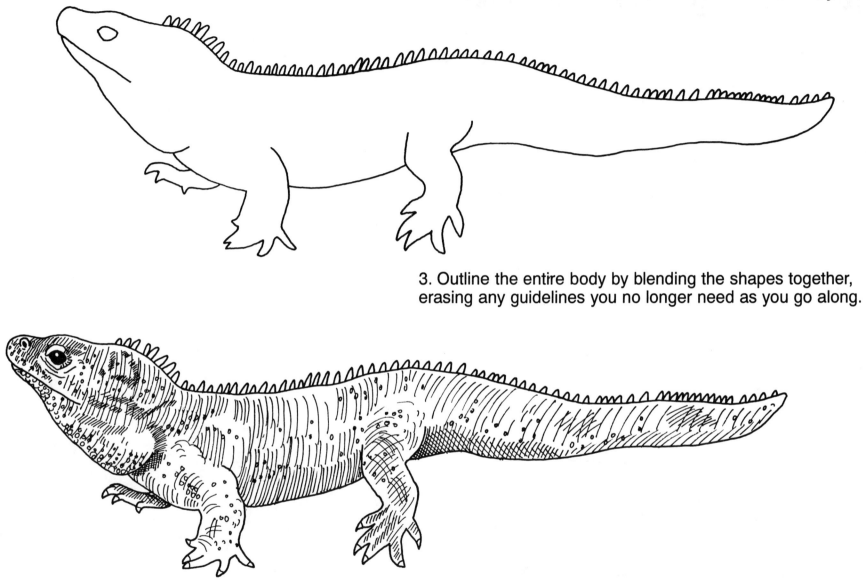

3. Outline the entire body by blending the shapes together, erasing any guidelines you no longer need as you go along.

4. Add details and some light shading, and watch your finished drawing come alive!

If you're not satisfied with the way any part of your drawing looks, erase it and draw it again. Remember, practice makes perfect!

Giant Sable Antelope

These antelopes share the swampy African marshes with animals such as the hippopotamus, heron, and marsh mongoose. They are all part of an ecosystem.

Helpful Hint:
Sometimes a drawing may seem too hard to do. Just break it down, step by step, into simple guideline shapes. With practice, you'll soon be able to draw any animal, no matter how difficult it seems at first.

1. Start with the ovals for the shoulder and hindquarter, and connect them with curved lines, as shown. Add an oval for the head and a circle for the snout. Then add the eye and ears.

2. Add the guideline shapes for the legs, hooves, and tail. Then add the long, curved horns.

Remember to draw these guidelines lightly. They will be easier to erase as you refine and complete your picture.

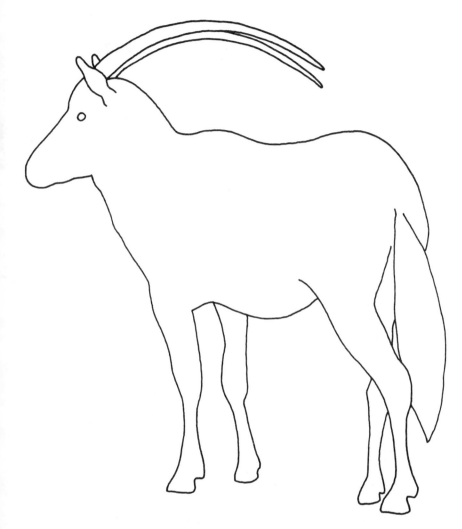

4. Use shading, texture, and any other details to complete your drawing.

Flash fact: Hunters have greatly depleted giant sable antelope numbers.

3. Erase any guidelines you no longer need as you blend the shapes into a smooth outline of the animal.

Golden Lion Tamarin

The golden lion tamarin has lost much of its South American rain forest habitat. Probably only several hundred remain in the wild.

Note: There are many overlapping shapes required to complete this picture. Remember, no matter how complicated an image appears, you'll be able to draw it if you break it down into simple steps.

2. Add guidelines for the eyes, nose, and mouth, and all the additional shapes for the legs and long, flowing tail.

1. Begin with a large free-form guideline shape for the body and an oval for the monkey's head. Within that oval draw another one for the face with two triangular ears on top of it.

3. Carefully erase any guidelines that you no longer need as you blend and refine the shapes and lines. Pay close attention to the way the mane sits on top of the tamarin's head.

4. Complete the facial features. Then add shading and other details to the mane and body. The tamarin's mane is a bright golden-orange, which gets darker further down the body.

When you're completely satisfied with the way your drawing looks, begin adding the finishing touches.

Flash fact: Due to successful breeding programs in zoos worldwide, there are more of these monkeys living in zoos than in the wild.

Peregrine Falcon

The falcon preys on other birds, gulls, pigeons, and ducks. A real acrobat, it will dive from extraordinary heights, sail at high speeds, and capture its prey on the wing.

1. Start by drawing a large oval, slightly pointed at the bottom end for the body. Then draw a similar oval inside the first one for the wing. Add a small overlapping oval for the head, a circle for the eye, and two small triangles for the beak.

2. Add two triangles and a long oval for the tail feathers. Then add the other basic shapes for the legs and feet.

Remember to draw these guidelines lightly. They will be easier to erase as you refine and complete your picture.

106

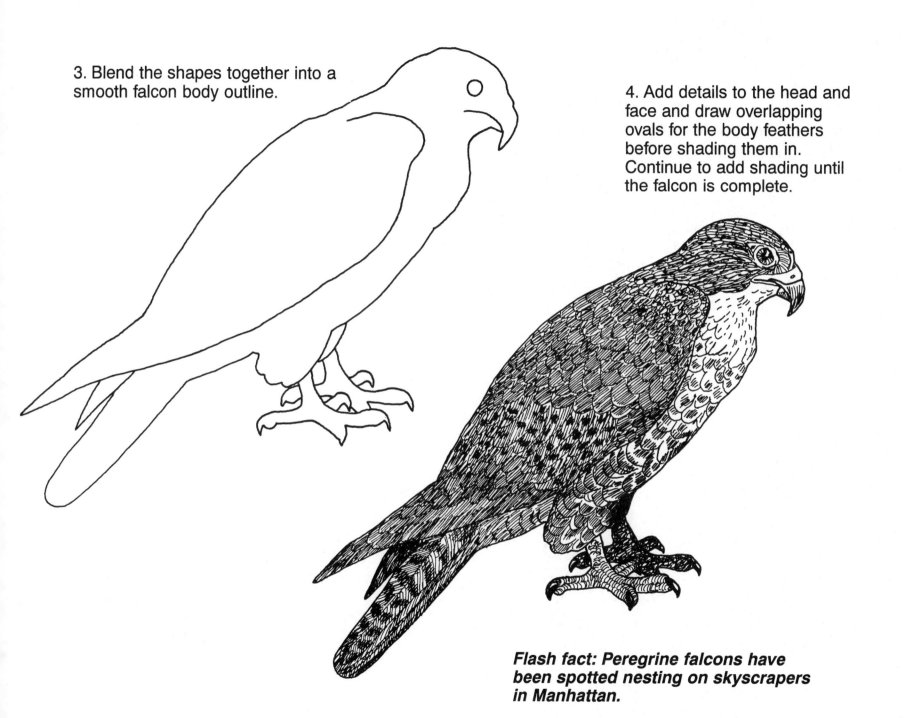

3. Blend the shapes together into a smooth falcon body outline.

4. Add details to the head and face and draw overlapping ovals for the body feathers before shading them in. Continue to add shading until the falcon is complete.

Flash fact: Peregrine falcons have been spotted nesting on skyscrapers in Manhattan.

Grevy's Zebra

This East African creature is the largest of all zebras. Its narrow-striped coat makes it a target for poachers who sell animal skins.

1. Start by drawing the large, irregular, oval-shaped body. Add another oval for the head and connect it to the body, forming the neck. Add another guideline on top of the neck to form the mane. Draw a small circle for the snout, and two triangular shapes for the ears.

2. Carefully add the legs, hooves, and tail. Remember to keep your guidelines lightly drawn.

Note: This is a very important step. It establishes the basic overall structure and look of your drawing. In steps 3 and 4, you are simply refining and adding details to the figure you have created in steps 1 and 2.

Flash fact: About 15,000 Grevy's zebras are still living in the wild.

3. Blend all the shapes into a smooth zebra outline, erasing any lines you no longer need as you go along.

4. Complete the eyes, ears, nose, and mouth, and add the zebra's beautiful stripes. Add some shading, and when you're done, draw some other African animals into a scene with the zebra.

Right Whale

The right whale got its name from whalers, because it was the "right" whale to hunt. It lives close to shore, is a slow swimmer, and contains lots of oil.

Note: Always draw your guidelines lightly in steps 1 and 2. It will be easier to change or erase them later.

1. Start with a lightly drawn, huge oval guideline shape for the body and a smaller one for the front fin. Add a small eye and a rectangular shape for the head. Connect the head to the body.

2. Draw the whale's tail by first sketching two wavy triangular shapes, joined at the bottom. Connect this shape to the rear of the whale's body. Then add long curvy lines on the front of the whale as guidelines for the mouth.

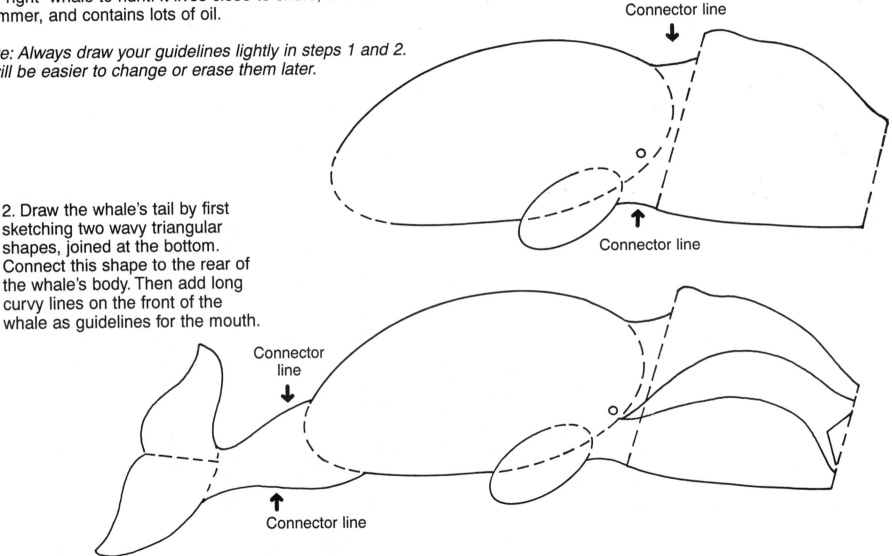

Connector line

Connector line

Connector line

Connector line

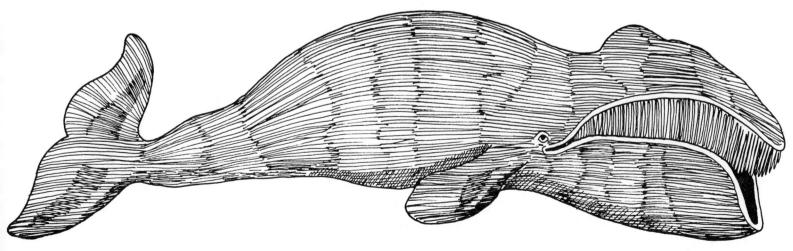

3. Blend the shapes, erasing unnecessary guidelines as you go along, into a smooth outline of the entire whale.

Flash fact: Unlike other whales, the right whale has two blowholes. When it comes up for air, it blows water out in two directions.

4. Add light, horizontal shading along the body. Use straight vertical lines to draw the baleen in the whale's mouth. The baleen acts like a filter, sifting tiny sea creatures from the water for the whale to eat.

Whooping Crane

These cranes live in the marshlands of North America. By 1941, hunting and marsh drainage had reduced their numbers in the wild to fewer than 20.

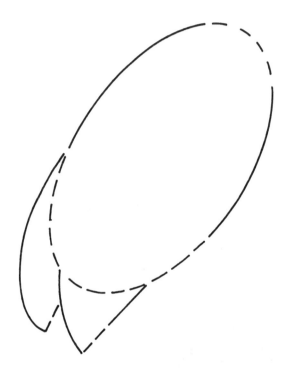

2. Add an oval and triangular beak for the head. Connect the head to the body, forming the long, slender neck. Note how one of the connecting lines extends to the top of the right leg. Add the long legs and use a series of triangular shapes to form the feet.

1. Start by drawing a large oval for the crane's body. Then draw the two basic shapes for the tail feathers.

Remember to draw these guidelines lightly. They will be easier to erase as you refine and complete your picture.

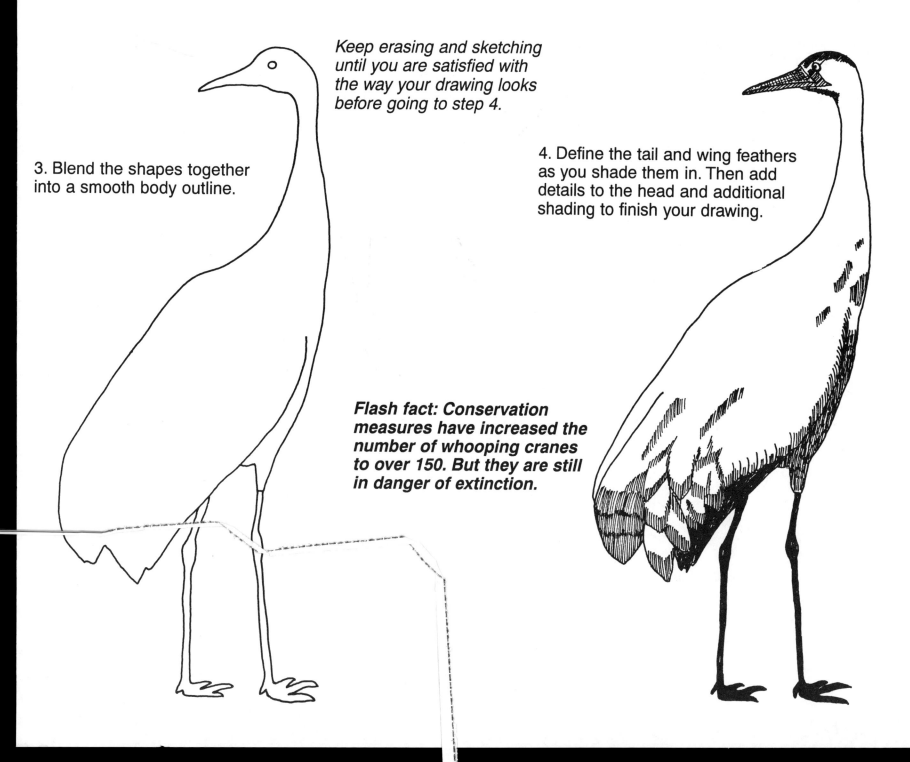

Keep erasing and sketching until you are satisfied with the way your drawing looks before going to step 4.

3. Blend the shapes together into a smooth body outline.

4. Define the tail and wing feathers as you shade them in. Then add details to the head and additional shading to finish your drawing.

Flash fact: Conservation measures have increased the number of whooping cranes to over 150. But they are still in danger of extinction.

113

Orangutan

The trees of Borneo and Sumatra—home to the orangutan—
are being cut down for timber. The forests are disappearing,
and the orangutans along with them.

Helpful Hint
*Sometimes a drawing may seem too hard to do. Just break it
down, step by step, into simple guideline shapes. With practice, you'll soon be able to draw any animal, no matter how
difficult it seems at first.*

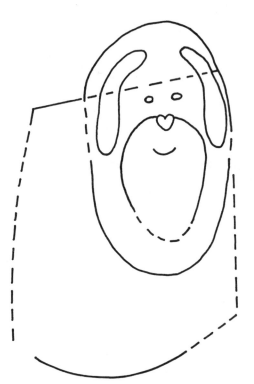

1. Begin with a basic oval
shape for the head. Within
it, draw a smaller one. Add
the eyes, mouth, a small
heart-shaped nose, and
two bent oval shapes on
either side of the eyes.
Then draw a rounded, boxy
shape for the body.

2. Carefully add the additional guideline shapes
for the arms, hands, legs, and feet. This may
appear complicated at first, so sketch the limbs
lightly, one at a time, until you have it right.

3. Combine and blend the shapes into an outline drawing of the ape. Note how the outline is shaggy in some places to represent the orangutan's long hairs.

Flash fact: In the language spoken on the island of Borneo, "orangutan" means "man who lives in the forest."

4. Now finish your drawing by adding all the details. For a more realistic look, use a black or dark orange felt-tip pen to add the orangutan's shaggy hair.

115

Clouded Leopard

This big, yellowish-gray cat lives in the forests and swamps of Asia. It hunts by night, but is also hunted by people for its beautiful spotted coat.

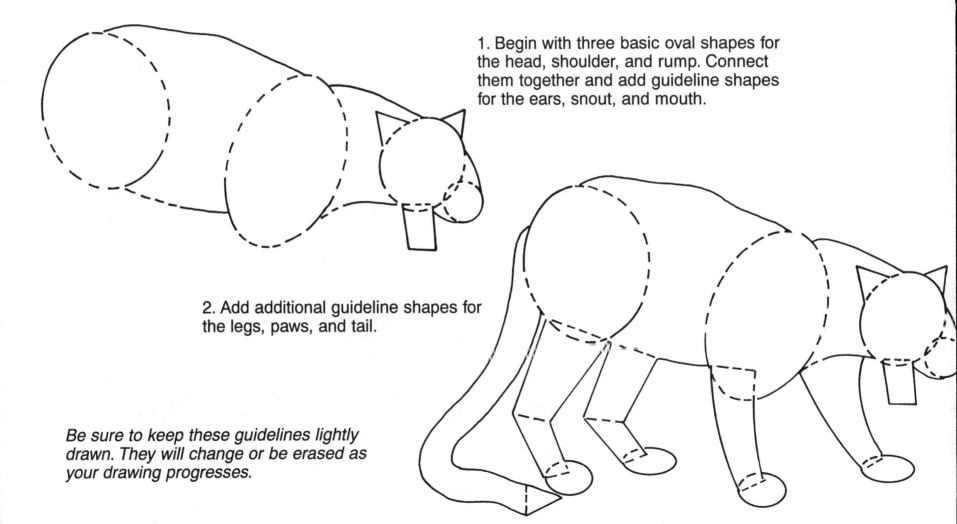

1. Begin with three basic oval shapes for the head, shoulder, and rump. Connect them together and add guideline shapes for the ears, snout, and mouth.

2. Add additional guideline shapes for the legs, paws, and tail.

Be sure to keep these guidelines lightly drawn. They will change or be erased as your drawing progresses.

3. Blend and shape all the forms together, paying close attention to how all the shapes and lines interconnect. When you're satisfied with the way the leopard's outline looks, start adding details.

4. Complete the facial features and other details. Finally, carefully draw the leopard's spectacular, spotted coat.

Flash fact: This cat has especially long canine teeth and a fierce look, but cannot roar. The clouded leopard is a purring cat.

117

Estuarine Saltwater Crocodile

Long hunted for its valuable hide, this crocodile can grow as long as 23 feet. It's the world's biggest reptile. Now protected, it can be found all over southeastern Asia.

Helpful Hint
Sometimes a drawing may seem too hard to do. Just break it down, step by step, into simple guideline shapes. With practice, you'll soon be able to draw any animal, no matter how difficult it seems at first.

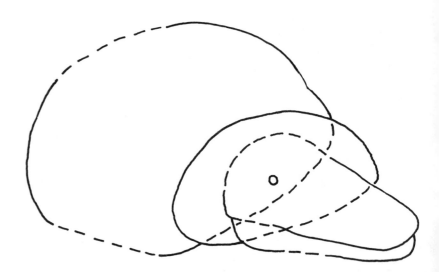

1. Start your sketch with a large free-form oval for the crocodile's body. Next, add a smaller overlapping oval for the thick neck. Then add the basic shapes for the head and jaws, and a small circle for the eye.

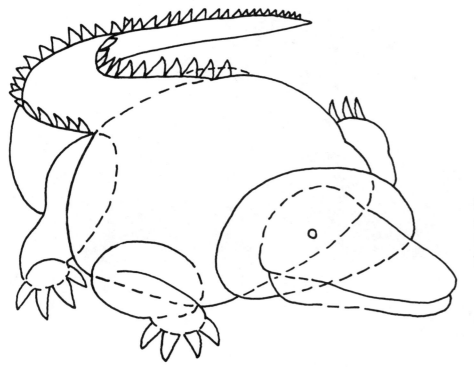

2. Draw the long powerful, tail. Then add a series of little triangles along the top of it. Using simple basic shapes, like ovals and triangles, create the legs and claws.

Make sure you have built a solid foundation with the first two steps before continuing.

Flash fact: Northern Australia is one of the few places where crocodile populations are increasing.

3. Combine all the shapes, erasing guidelines as you go along. Now you're ready for the finishing touches.

4. Complete the eye and head. Note the bumpy ridges on the head and neck, and the rows of smaller ridges running along the crocodile's back. Finally, add lots of scales, texture, and shading to complete your drawing.

Copper Butterfly

This European butterfly lives in wet marshlands that are shrinking due to land drainage for farming.

Flash fact: The copper butterfly is considered extinct in Great Britain and is seldom seem in the rest of Europe.

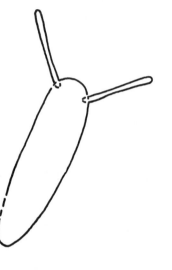

1. Start by lightly sketching an oval guideline shape for the body. Add two thin shapes for the antennae.

2. Lightly sketch two overlapping triangular shapes for the front wings and the other shapes for the back wings.

3. Blend the guideline shapes into a clean outline of the butterfly, erasing any lines you no longer need.

4. Add lines, details, and shading as shown. The butterfly's body is brown and its wings are bright orange with black trimming along the edges.

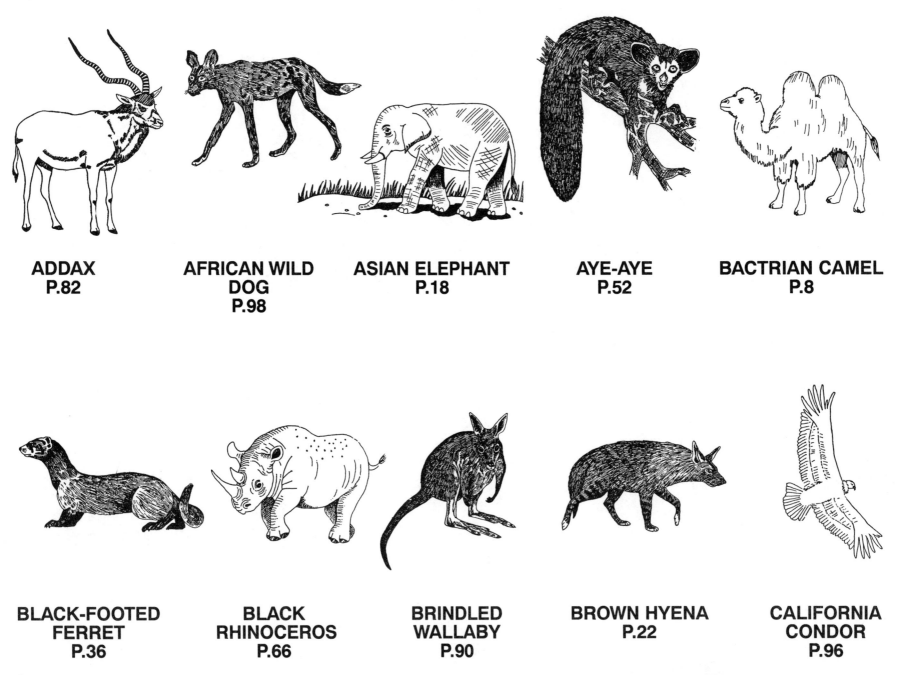

ADDAX
P.82

AFRICAN WILD
DOG
P.98

ASIAN ELEPHANT
P.18

AYE-AYE
P.52

BACTRIAN CAMEL
P.8

BLACK-FOOTED
FERRET
P.36

BLACK
RHINOCEROS
P.66

BRINDLED
WALLABY
P.90

BROWN HYENA
P.22

CALIFORNIA
CONDOR
P.96

CHEETAH
P.34

CHIMPANZEE
P.56

**CLOUDED
LEOPARD
P.116**

**COPPER
BUTTERFLY
P.121**

**DALMATIAN
PELICAN
P.94**

**ESKIMO CURLEW
P.16**

**ESTUARINE
SALTWATER
CROCODILE
P.118**

**FIJIAN BANDED
IGUANA
P.42**

**GALPAGOS
TURTLE
P.97**

**GIANT ANTEATER
P.12**

GIANT ARMADILLO
P.44

GIANT OTTER
P.74

GIANT PANDA
P.14

GIANT SABLE
ANTELOPE
P.102

GOLDEN LION
TAMARIN
P.104

GREVY'S ZEBRA
P.108

HAWAIIAN GOOSE
P.38

HAWKSBILL SEA
TURTLE
P.88

HELMETED
HORNBILL
P.48

HUMPBACK
WHALE
P.40

INDIAN PYTHON
P.84

INDGO MACAW
P.58

INDRI
P.54

IVORY BILLED
WOODPECKER
P.76

JAGUAR
P.60

KOMODO DRAGON
P.20

LEATHERBACK
SEA TURTLE
P.50

MALAYAN TAPIR
P.24

MEDITERRANEAN
MONK SEAL
P.33

MOUNTAIN
GORILLA
P.30

**NORTHERN
SPOTTED OWL
P.32**

**NUMBAT
P.26**

**ORANGUTAN
P.114**

**PEREGRINE
FALCON
P.106**

**PROBOSCIS
MONKEY
P.86**

**PRZEWALSKI'S
HORSE
P.70**

**QUEEN
ALEXANDRA'S
BIRDWING
P.68**

**RED WOLF
P.28**

**RESPLENDENT
QUETZAL
P.62**

**RIGHT WHALE
P.110**

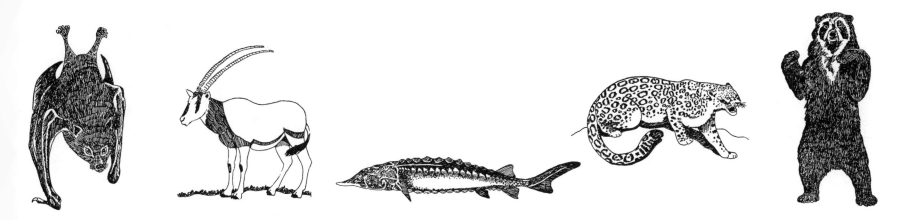

**RODRIGUES
FLYING FOX
P.78**

**SCIMITAR-HORNED
ORYX
P.46**

**SHORTNOSE
STURGEON
P.72**

**SNOW
LEOPARD
P.80**

**SPECTACLED
BEAR
P.64**

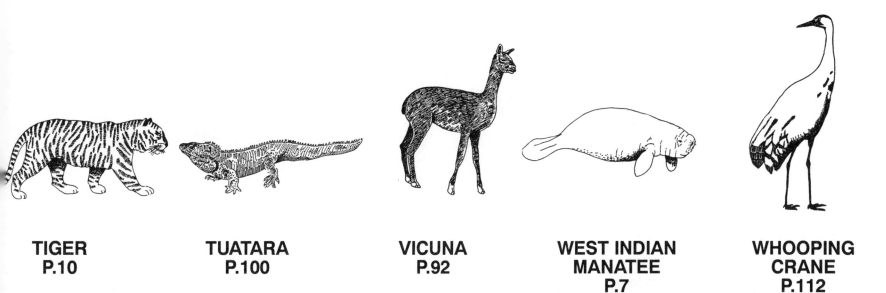

**TIGER
P.10**

**TUATARA
P.100**

**VICUNA
P.92**

**WEST INDIAN
MANATEE
P.7**

**WHOOPING
CRANE
P.112**